Moving Forward in Faith

LET'S GO!

DEBORAH J. ANDREWS

LET'S GO! MOVING FORWARD IN FAITH
Copyright © 2025 by Deborah J. Andrews

All rights reserved. Neither this publication nor any part of this publication may be reproduced or transmitted in any form or by any means, electronic or mechanical, including photocopying, recording or any information storage and retrieval system, without permission in writing from the author.

Scripture quotations taken from the New King James Version®. Copyright © 1982 by Thomas Nelson. Used by permission. All rights reserved.

ISBN: 978-1-4866-2509-3
eBook ISBN: 978-1-4866-2510-9

Word Alive Press
119 De Baets Street Winnipeg, MB R2J 3R9
www.wordalivepress.ca

Cataloguing in Publication information can be obtained from Library and Archives Canada.

Are you ready to embark on a journey beyond what's comfortable, to deepen your faith and embrace the unseen? Walking by faith, not by sight? (2 Cor. 5:7) As I delved into this book, I was amazed by how God began speaking to me with uncanny clarity... With each page I turned, His presence seemed to grow. This isn't just a book; it's a living faith journey where the Holy Spirit will meet you.

I believe Deborah's book will inspire and challenge you to deepen your faith, relationship, and trust in God, putting actionable steps to your faith so it truly comes alive.

You'll be on the edge of your seat as you dive into the stories, insights, and reflections within these pages, guiding you toward a deeper relationship with God and encouraging you to grow in your faith. Strap on your seatbelt—you're about to embark on an amazing ride as you open the pages of my friend Deborah's book!"

—Katarina Watson, Christian Life-Coach,
Advanced Kinesiologist/Massage Therapist

A sincere, heartfelt account of a journey of faith that I found to be both challenging and inspiring. This book will encourage you in your faith, and Deborah's story will show you that with God, all things are possible!
—Alison Spriggs, Author, *Knitting Makes You Fat, The Real Owners of Skye*

Deborah J. Andrews is a water-walker. This book encourages you to trust even when you can't see the next step. It will inspire you to take that step and get out of the boat, like Peter did, and water-walk.

—Rev. Pauline Glover, Weddings I DO Officiant

The Bible makes it clear that every follower of Christ must walk by faith and live by faith. It even goes further to say that without faith, it's impossible to please God. If the Word of God declares it is impossible, we can be assured it truly is. Faith is really that important.

Deborah takes you on a journey of discovering the life of faith through personal hardships to victories, both small and great. Her story exemplifies the often-quoted statement, "Faith makes things possible, but not easy." Be encouraged as you walk through the pages of this book, and let her journey encourage and increase your own faith.

—Dr. Dick Deweert, President, Dominion Broadcasting and co-host of *Lifeline Today* national TV program, Founder and Senior Leader of Third Day Victory Church in Lethbridge, Alberta

God's love and purpose as she (Deborah J. Andrews), like Abraham, follows the Lord in full surrender and unshakable faith. She is gold refined in fire and this book will bless you, inspiring courage to believe and trust through uncertainty.

—Cathryn Nash, One of the Founding Pastors, Frontline Church; Prophetic Conference Leader

Lovingly Dedicated To:

The extraordinary memory of a faithful and courageous man, a loving and compassionate father who fought the good fight and kept the faith.

And to my mother, a strong and beautiful person who never ceased to believe in me, even when forsaken by so many others.

I am also forever grateful to my compassionate, generous, faith-filled husband, Kevin. I can't imagine having lived this out-of-the-box life with anyone else, and my heart is full to overflowing as I think of how he and our three kids walked this faith journey together with me.

You, my children, are as they say, my heart walking around outside of my body.

I love and treasure you all more than words could ever say!

Contents

Acknowledgements	ix
Foreword	xi
Introduction	xiii
ONE: A Willing Participant	1
TWO: Discovering Faith	15
THREE: Holding on to Faith	31
FOUR: Growing in Faith	51
FIVE: Trouble with Faith	69
SIX: Radical Faith	87
SEVEN: Moving Forward in Faith	105
EIGHT: Strategies in Faith	123
NINE: Faith That Overcomes	143
TEN: Rewards of Faith	163
ELEVEN: Active Faith	175
TWELVE: Understanding Faith	189
Conclusion: Life of Faith	203
Appendix I: Sons of Thunder Prophecy	211
Appendix II: The Gospel: A Love Story	219
Also by Deborah J. Andrews:	223

Acknowledgements

Throughout the adventure of living and writing this story, a number of people and organizations stepped in to partner with the Lord in what He was doing in and through us. There were also people who lent a helping hand to our family during times of great need. I am overwhelmed and filled with such gratitude as I think of each and every one of you. We truly couldn't have done it without you!

To all who read the manuscript and provided valuable input or a heartfelt endorsement—thank you!

To Laura, Bee and family, I am humbled and blessed by the extravagant kindness extended me in facilitating and realizing the audiobook version of *Let's Go!*

And finally, a HUGE shout out to my brilliant and generous brother, who not only played a significant role in the logistics of getting us to Scotland but also in providing insightful and godly wisdom in the reviewing of this manuscript. My love and appreciation run deep.

Foreword

I am delighted to recommend to you the remarkable journey captured within the pages of *Let's Go! Moving Forward in Faith*. From the very first chapter, you'll find yourself drawn into a narrative that is as gripping as it is inspirational. Deborah takes us on a soul-stirring journey of faith, courage, and trust in God. Through trials and triumphs, challenges and victories, Deborah shares the highs and lows of her journey, reminding us all that the path of faith is not always easy, but it's always worth it.

What truly sets this book apart is its authenticity. With honesty and vulnerability, Deborah invites us into her innermost thoughts and struggles, offering not just a glimpse into her journey but a roadmap for our own. Through her experiences, we learn that faith isn't just about belief; it's about action, obedience, and surrendering to a plan greater than our own.

Let's Go! is more than just a book; it's a reminder that no matter how daunting the journey may seem, we are never alone. It reminds us of the truth that when we put our trust in God, all things are possible. Miracles can and do happen!

So to all of you who seek inspiration, encouragement, and a sense of purpose, I wholeheartedly recommend this book.

Corri Hunsperger
Producer/Co-host of *Talk Truth*

Introduction

I was just a wee lass—perhaps about two years old—when our family of four nestled into our station wagon for one of our fun-filled expeditions out on the open road. We were wending our way down the highway with my very capable, always safe, defensive-driving dad at the wheel. My baby brother, who was seated beside me in the back, was upset about something, so Mom had turned around to help him. Of course, back in those days there were no seatbelts, so Mom was actually on her knees, facing the back.

Out of the blue, there was a significant jolt, causing my mom to falter. She glanced over at my dad, who was visibly shaken—actually, white as a sheet. He stammered, "Look out the back." She did and was utterly confounded by what she saw.

There, across both lanes, was a semi-trailer truck. As my parents struggled to assimilate what had just taken place, my dad choked out, "That was just in front of us." The semi had literally jack-knifed IN FRONT of us and was now BEHIND us!

With cut-out hillside on both sides that would not have allowed for a path around the semi, we had just experienced a lifesaving miracle. We were safe, untouched, and unharmed, apparently trans-located and protected—not a scratch on the car or on any of us!

Something about this event and subsequent others demonstrated to me that God had a plan and a purpose for me. I just didn't know what that plan was! Throughout my early years, I did live *with* faith, but as I would later learn, I was not living *by* faith. That came down the line when I more fully grasped the concept of what it was to fully yield to the Father. This revelation propelled me toward a willingness to go, do, and be whatever was asked of me. *This* was when everything changed!

It wasn't long after I laid it all down that I received my first assignment, and boy, did I feel ill-prepared. With no theological training, a busy family life, work commitments, and extremely limited resources, I had no idea how I was to accomplish what was being asked of me. Regardless, there was a job to be done, and I had the choice to obey or not. I chose to obey and so began a modern-day faith adventure, living the life of an ordinary person blessed with that which is out-of-the-ordinary because of faith in an extraordinary God.

The "call" was to bring *His* music into the world. Now that's a tall order! Although bewildered as to precisely how to do that, I stepped out and into a very steep learning curve. With our Heavenly Father at the helm, I gathered hundreds and thousands of people together for large-scale gospel concerts in mainstream venues at a time when events such as these were usually only held in churches or at youth events. Other assignments followed, each one carrying with them greater risk and sacrifice, until the day we received the biggest "ask" of all.

My husband and I were required to dig deeper than ever before. We were being asked to leave all that was familiar behind. In faith and obedience, we, and our three children, left our home and life in Canada and moved to Scotland, not knowing a single person there, with no visible means of support and no idea why we were being sent. It was us and God, and that's it.

"It was the best of times. It was the worst of times." But in the end, what ensued was nothing short of miraculous as God connected us with others who had done the same as us! Once in Scotland, we and our God-assembled team received direction largely through dreams and visions. What a ride! Like a roller coaster, the "highs" were unlike anything you could ever imagine: exhilarating, inspiring, and rewarding. And the "lows," painful and difficult.

I've often been asked how I mustered up the courage to live this kind of a life, and I'd have to say, it was it was a fairly gradual process. I didn't jump into the deep end of the faith pool my first time out. I started at the shallow end, building skill, knowledge, and muscle so that, over time, my faith had increased to a place of complete surrender. I became like Isaiah who when he heard the voice of the Lord say, "*Whom shall I send, and who will go ...*" replied, "*Here am I! Send me*" (Isaiah 6:8). It has been about choosing to be a willing and obedient participant in the life God has ordained for me. Nothing less will do.

I've learned that this decision to walk by faith requires both an unwavering commitment to Him *and* a compliant and flexible approach to life. It means operating outside of our comfort zones, and it expects a willful "death" to self. Once postured in this completely deliberate position of humility, we need to accept that we will experience discomfort. This is a given when choosing to live in a manner that is completely contrary to the way of the world.

I've had to remind myself that just as God didn't bring the Israelites through the desert for death to overtake them, neither did He direct us without a purpose and a plan. God never changes.

> God remains the same,
> regardless of what's going on in our lives or in our world.

Running the race of faith is definitely not for the faint of heart, yet it's for everyone. It's for you. It's for me. There are benefits and challenges in choosing this life. It's not a one-time event but rather a life-long marathon. What's astonishing, though, are the stories that result. When God is in control, our stories become testimonies that inspire, challenge, and change us.

I hope my story will bless, excite, and encourage you. Yes, there is most definitely a cost in following. There is also a cost in not following. I have chosen to go with God, and I hope that you will too!

LET'S GO! Moving forward in faith.

ONE
A Willing Participant

HERE AND NOW

As I begin to share my journey of faith with you, I am in the "valley." You probably know, understand, and have experienced the valley. It's that place where things are *not* going as planned. Life isn't progressing the way we'd hoped, and we can see that for a time we'll be residing in that dreaded place of pain, growth, and disappointment.

Typically, one wouldn't venture out and share their story *while* in this condition. It would seem ludicrous to even attempt to impart words of wisdom or encouragement amidst personal pain and turmoil. After all, how can an average person with troubles of her own have anything noteworthy to say? Well, simply put, it's not so much about what *I* have to say but rather about what *God* wants to say to you, through me. Although I haven't realized absolute victory apparent in having climbed the highest mountain, followed every rainbow—gotta love *The Sound of Music*—and … you get the picture. But for some reason, He has chosen to use *me,* just as I am, to encourage *you*!

God wants me to share with you, from this place of humility and brokenness, what it is to have faith in the difficult days.

He wants you to hear His truths from someone who isn't currently jumping for joy in a mountaintop experience. He wants you to know that He loves you and will never leave you or forsake you, and He wants you to hear that from one who must remind herself of this every day.

Sometimes it can be challenging to believe that these promises are true, but I've come to know that despite my circumstances, God remains the same. So it is in Him, and in His Word, that I place my trust. I cannot trust my feelings. I can only trust Him.

Sadly, few people understand this journey of faith, so it has been an excruciatingly lonely walk. As a result of each faith step that my husband, Kevin, and I have been asked to take, we have lost very dear friends. These are people who didn't understand what God was asking of us and definitely didn't want to walk the road with us. Through it all, though, I've had an undeniable sense of purpose and determination that has propelled me upward, onward, and toward the goal, allowing me to run the race.

Hopefully it won't be long before I emerge from this valley, but in the meantime, there's apparently still a great deal that I must learn while here. So I'll do the only thing I know how to do, which is to fix my eyes and heart on the Lord, seeking His face, and remain on my knees. There have been tough days before, and there will be difficult days ahead. Numerous people have stories far more troublesome than ours, and some aren't nearly as bad, but the bottom line is this: when you're in the valley, it's really not fun.

> Pain is pain. Heartache is heartache. Loss is loss.
> Trying to judge another's pain is futile at best
> and cruel at worst.

January 1, 2008. Typically the first day of a new year is a day of new beginnings, fresh determination, and hopeful anticipation of all the future holds. But today, for me, it's a day of utter desolation. Broken and crying out to God, I feel as though my heart has been shattered into a million little pieces. Our financial resources are nil. We literally have absolutely nothing with which to live. Our teenage children also have nothing because they've contributed all their savings in order to pay our rent.

I am sickened to the core by this new "low." Without a vehicle, the five of us walk, take the bus, or accept rides from generous folks. Attending meetings or functions is challenging, and grocery shopping, when we have the funds for it, is downright painful, especially when considering the arduous trek home, usually executed in a rainy clime. Our furniture, dishes, and clothing are "tired," and we're continually fighting issues of mould in our home, something that's particularly challenging given that I suffer from an auto-immune disease and a vast number of allergies.

We live in a foreign country because just over three months ago, God sent us away from our homeland, family, and friends to a nation halfway across the world, to a place we'd never been, where we didn't know even one person, and He hasn't informed us as to why—yet.

Just over four weeks ago, my very precious dad—a hero of the faith and a hero of mine—passed away after having been diagnosed with cancer only two days after we arrived in this new land. Our days and nights have been filled with mourning this loss and coping with the pain of leaving my mom. Our surroundings are unfamiliar, and we frequently need to battle the depression and oppression that permeates the country to which we've been sent. We have our faith and we have one another, and that's it. God has stripped us, emptied us, and removed us.

Although today is a difficult day, I'm clinging to the hope of tomorrow. I know that with God leading me in His gentle and compassionate way, I will eventually find my way up the rocky terrain, joyfully breathing in that mountaintop experience, having grown and experienced a fresh wind of God in my life by way of a broken spirit and a contrite heart.

For some reason, today God wants me to share with you in this place of brokenness what it is to have faith in the difficult days. He wants you to know the possibilities that lay ahead of you and that although you too may be in the valley, it's possible to move outside the confines of your own pain and add value to the life of another. This is something that I hope to do for you through my story.

As I look back on my walk, I can see how and why God has led me down this path in the ways He has. I can see how blessed I've been to live a life of purpose and passion. Naturally we have those moments when we observe our lives through a more "worldly" lens, and from that perspective, things may appear quite grim. This is why we ought to view our lives as God does—pleased with who we have become and filled with hope by all that we are yet to be. He sees the potential and the possibilities that lie within us, not the flaws and culpabilities.

Like the gentleman He is, He patiently waits for us to discover who we are in Him. He stands at the gate like the father of the prodigal son, in anticipation that soon we will be home—not perfect, not rich, but with a renewed understanding of His strength and how desperately we need Him to accomplish anything of substance.

> Right here and now, we can do mighty exploits for Him,
> knowing that in and of ourselves, it was impossible.
> But with God, ALL things are possible.

Choosing a life of faith can prove challenging, especially for those who need to overcome an opposing spiritual background, upbringing, or training. It may even require a major overhaul of one's thought life to release incorrect teaching or legalistic beliefs from the past and open ourselves to a new way of thinking. In allowing Christ to rule and reign in our hearts, it's imperative that we also give Him access to our heads, our minds.

By nature, humans are generally resistant to change and uncomfortable looking at life and faith from a new perspective. Sometimes we become trapped or entrenched in teaching that binds us and makes it next to impossible for us to break free. What amazes me is that we Christians expect agnostics, scientists, Muslims, Buddhists, or even our own unsaved friends to look beyond and outside their teaching, yet we refuse to seek God and Jesus beyond what we've been taught. Ouch! That one may have stung, but it needed to be said.

Rest assured that although we may not have all the answers or know what tomorrow holds, we do know *who* holds tomorrow. With that in mind, I am certain God, the maker of heaven and earth, is more than able to accomplish what concerns us today.

While remaining firm in Christ and in the Word of God, we must also endeavour to remain "open" to the possibility that we may have gotten some things wrong. While one church or ministry leader could espouse a certain belief, that same "core value" might be completely dismissed by another institution. Who's right? Usually we believe that the truth resides with the one we're following, which is why we've "bought into" that particular body of believers. However, this can also prove dangerous.

We should only follow Christ. We should only align ourselves with Christ. This way, even if our leaders are off-track or go astray, we're still hearing from, and in line with, our Lord.

I stand before you not as an expert or one to follow but as a regular woman with some undeniably real experiences. My understanding is based solely on the Word of God, revelation as I know it today, and guidance as given by the Holy Spirit and the wise counsel of those on similar journeys.

As I said before, the ride has sometimes been rough, and on occasion it's seemed as though my Lord, my knight in shining armour, hasn't arrived on time or in the ways and means I was hoping, but He always has come through for me. Not only that, but the results are usually a lot better than anything I could've ever imagined.

We recognize that much of what we've been asked to do is prophetic. We are pioneers. Our story is simply a foreshadowing of what is to come, a way to provide insight and encouragement to those who will follow. We actually identify more closely with a group considerably younger than ourselves. My hope is that our story will give this group a road map of sorts and provide their circumspect parents with knowledge and understanding.

Although we appreciate and acknowledge the reason for this "call," it doesn't change the fact that when I first began to write my story, I was nearly fifty, my husband was almost sixty, and we were in the position of "starting over." Our peer group seems to be continually shaking their heads and rolling their eyes whenever our names are mentioned. The emotional roller coaster associated with this life of faith and my personal battles with illness have also taken their toll. While things from a worldly perspective look a little ominous, surprisingly we have remained optimistic. We still possess a youthful drive, determination, willingness, passion, and hope for all the future holds.

The key to having achieved this attitude is in continually reminding ourselves to *not* look at our situation with human eyes. While this can be extraordinarily difficult to accomplish, I am determined to measure my life based on how my Heavenly Father views me rather than through the eyes of those who judge me. It's when I see things with fleshly eyes, as the world would view me, that my life appears bleak at best. This is the key, though! I need to remain focused on things above. I need to maintain a spiritual perspective.

> It requires a lot of work and discipline to see things from God's perspective, especially when the earthly vantage point is continually before me.

It should have been a relatively simple task, yet as a result of the heavy grocery bags lining my hands and arms, welts and a distasteful array of rashes began to emerge on my skin. I was trying to keep my mind off the obvious discomfort when my thoughts inadvertently meandered back to a simpler time.

These memories didn't placate me but merely reminded me of the insanity of my current situation. It was strange to me that I was finding solace in recalling films I'd seen of African women carrying buckets of food and water on their heads for miles and miles in the hot sun. I reprimanded myself for thinking such thoughts and wondered why we must focus on someone worse off than ourselves in order to be consoled. Ah, the human condition in all its complexities.

I was shaken back into reality as one of my plastic bags broke and a package of strawberries tumbled across the sidewalk. I put everything down, scrambling to pick up as many of the berries as possible, all the while re-organizing the shopping so that it would fit into one less bag. I pushed aside thoughts of how I must appear to passersby. No matter how you sliced it, this was highly unusual—a skilled, career-oriented, mature North American woman carrying food for a family of five, all alone, via bus and then up a steep and seemingly never-ending hill in the pouring rain to home, with so little money that not one bit of food could be lost! I couldn't recall signing up for this. Still, the physical part of the escapade had been the easy part.

The trying times had been the countless hours and days previous to this spent in desperate and anguished prayer, waiting and believing for our empty cupboards to be filled. My heart hurt and the tears flowed freely.

So how did I get to this place? Well, let's start at the very beginning, a very good place to start—*The Sound of Music* again?

My story is unique, just as your story is unique. That in and of itself is incredible to me; our stories can be so different, yet as long as the destination is Christ, we all end up at the same place—living for Him, seeking after Him and His righteousness, and enjoying His blessings! Growing up in a Christian home, I learned early on that I was loved, special, and protected. I learned to pray, to read the Bible, and to obey the commandments. As I grew, I discovered that many others didn't share the same kind of life I did. They didn't have a supportive, encouraging mother and a gentle, prayer-filled father. Their lives were, in some cases, tragic.

This pained me, and out of compassion, I was able to "share" my parents with others who needed a taste of what my brother and I had in abundance. Although we weren't financially wealthy, we also never seemed to be in need.

Days before turning age twelve, I made the decision to follow Christ, with a resolve to serve Him for the rest of my life. Of course, this wouldn't always be the case, as I, like so many, would find myself at various stages in my walk stagnant, floundering, or simply off-track. Meeting my husband, Kevin, really started to bring me back to God. The more I shared the goodness of God with him, all that I had learned while growing up and what I knew to be true, the more this faith inside of me was renewed and began to bubble up again. I realized how much I missed this relationship with my Saviour and began to thank Him for never giving up on me.

After marrying, Kevin and I began to faithfully attend church, raised a family, worked, lived, and generally felt called to be salt and light, which I believe we were. Over time, though, I began an even deeper journey of faith, and what I encountered and learned along the way is what I would like to share with you here.

> This walk has taken some staggering twists and turns,
> beginning with seven significant words that
> forever changed my life.

With those words, God plucked me out of a stable job with the culture department in government and into an amazing adventure with Him. Since that time, I've been passionately committed to, and captivated by, the power of worship evangelism—be it organizing, managing, singing, producing, or directing large outreach concerts, events, and festivals. I've been blessed with opportunities to do prison ministry, street ministry, and uniquely mission-minded endeavours. It's been a phenomenal ride that's taken me to new depths and dimensions of this wondrous thing we call "faith."

WHAT IS FAITH?

So what exactly *is* faith? How is living *by* faith unlike living *with* faith? What's the difference between faith and religion? Why live a life of faith in a world that expresses such contempt toward those with a resolve to follow Christ? These are just a few of the many questions that could cause a person to shrink back in fear from choosing such a life. But I can tell you with all assurance that faith in Christ is life-changing, world-changing, and a decision that I would highly recommend.

A person of faith is one who is grounded in something much bigger, deeper, and more profound than self. The very word "faith" propels my thoughts to a place of peace, strength, power, and conviction. It motivates me to look beyond myself, my environment, and my circumstances.

When I speak of my faith to non-believers, they often assume that I'm "religious." But I am not "religious." I am filled with faith. This is considerably different. My faith isn't about law, system, structure, or traditions but rather relationship. My relationship with God, with Jesus, with the Holy Spirit is as real as any other relationship I have. My confidence, my trust are in my Lord. Yet while this faith is about relationship, its foundational principles are based on the Word of God, the Holy Bible. So what *does* the Bible say about faith? The most common definition is found in

Hebrews 11:1, which says, *"Now faith is the substance of things hoped for, the evidence of things not seen."*

This is a concept that can be difficult for us to get our minds around, but essentially it's saying that faith is about hope and beliefs and not about anything concrete or of this world. It's not something we can see or touch in the natural. It's spiritual. This is reiterated in 2 Corinthians 5:7, with Paul's simple explanation that:

"...we walk by faith, not by sight."

Although seemingly straightforward, it's a concept that is lost on many. If I were listening to a comedian speaking on this subject, I would picture him wryly but comically cajoling into his microphone: "What part of *not by sight* do you not get?" And when you think about it, he'd be absolutely correct. Somehow, a large percentage of the Christian community in particular has missed out on understanding what faith is all about. I think we've somehow come to believe that when we live by faith, it simply means we have a nice relationship with God, our family, and our church family, yet pretty much live the same way that everyone else in the world lives. Of course, we may attend church and do our best not to sin, and we try to do nice things for others, but on a day-to-day basis, we don't look too different from the world, and what's worse, people who do are considered to be strange and might even be subject to ridicule.

If faith is belief in and for something we can't see—and that's clearly scriptural—then why do we have such difficulty understanding our brothers and sisters who are called to do something out of the ordinary, something that may not be clearly defined or seem "realistic," as we understand reality to be?

We've confused *having* faith with living *by* faith.

When folks witness a true walk of faith, it doesn't necessarily "fit" with their understanding, ultimately making them feel very uncomfortable. This explains why those who criticize feel that not only should God's request make complete sense to them, but a comprehensive plan should be attached to that request. This sounds more like a business transaction than a call to action by the Almighty! But this is the way many have been taught to envisage faith. Because of this lack of understanding, not only are people often repelled by the very thought of what a person of faith is doing, but in some cases, they're even repelled by the actual person. I believe that what makes people so uncomfortable is the "unknown."

> It's the "not being able to see" part of the equation
> that bothers folks.
> But faith actually means not seeing.

As soon as we can see, it's really not faith any more, is it? Let me repeat that: once we can see, we're no longer operating in faith, because it's not only evident to us, but to everyone around us. When that happens, it's about seeing in the natural, and there's nothing supernatural or faith-like about that!

So many questions flooded my mind! How did I, a naïve, happy-go-lucky twenty-three-year-old singer, end up at the courthouse? Why is it that an innocent bystandar, such as myself, be compelled to testify? Must I reveal my identity by stating my name out loud for all to hear? Would the perpetrators or their friends come after me now that they knew who I was? Would I be safe?

This entire ordeal was the result of a dramatic robbery at a bank where I worked at the time. My passion was music, but I was, somewhat begrudgingly, working at the bank to pay the bills. Now here I was being asked to lay my life on the line and testify to what I had witnessed ...

The first I knew that anything out of the ordinary was taking place was when I heard a man shouting loudly at one of the tellers. I could immediately see that we were being robbed. This man was insistent and relentless, badgering the poor bank clerk until she passed out on the floor from fear.

Now that she was no longer able to provide him with the cash he was demanding, he leapt over the counter with a crazed look in his eyes. This meant there were no barriers of any kind between us and this out-of-control madman. He continued to yell and push employees out of his way, resulting in more staff passing out. I was positioned just a few feet away, standing by my desk. His back was to me, so in all the chaos, I did something I wasn't supposed to do. I slowly began to inch my way toward the alarm until I was abruptly startled into submission by a commanding voice hollering, "STOP! Don't move!" My heart leapt out of my chest as I twisted my head, only to see a sawed-off shotgun pointed at ME. Up until this point, I thought there was only one robber. I had no idea that TWO of them had entered the bank.

Strangely, the shock of this actually heightened and sharpened my senses, prompting my crisis training to kick into action. Although too terrified to look at the man holding the gun on me, I was determined to watch and memorize the other thief until they finally left the building. After their departure, the police arrived, followed by medical personnel to treat the traumatized staff that now littered the floor. I was one of the few still standing and, surprisingly, quite calm. Consequently, I was able to provide the police with a decent statement, recalling the staggering events that had ensued, along with a detailed description of one of the offenders.

Leaving work that day, I mistakenly thought that would be the end of it. Tragically, within days the thieves hit another bank and during their getaway struck a vehicle with a mom and a car-load of children. As a result of the impact, a small boy was killed. The criminals were captured in the process. As it turned out, my description perfectly matched one of these men, and this is how it came to pass that I was subpoenaed to testify.

The reason I tell you this story is because this event brought me to a crossroads. Here I was putting my life at risk for a job I found dry and boring, where they didn't offer me any support of any kind. Actually, they provided no counselling for any of us, and they didn't even give me the rest of the day off after I testified! This was not the first robbery I'd witnessed, just the worst. On top of that, my passion was music, so none of this "fit."

This incomprehensible event was the impetus I needed to take a step of faith and audition for my first professional production. And you know what? I got the job. It was only a three-month contract, but it was affirmation enough that I should both value myself and also follow my passion. It was risky but worth it, ultimately setting my life on a completely different trajectory. One that was more fitting.

These were just early days in learning how to step out of my comfort zone. I can't say I fully understood the magnitude of what stepping out in this way would do for me, but it most definitely built on the strong foundation that began in childhood. It reinforced the fact that I only had one life to live.

What's interesting is that when God asks us to do something in faith that others find strange and difficult to comprehend, there's almost always an undeniable certainty and conviction that comes within our spirit. There is a "knowing" that accompanies the request. It doesn't require the "calling" be something huge and earth-shattering. It could be anything. It could be a nudging of the Holy Spirit to take some time to pray or help someone in need. It could be a prompting to initiate spending time with a young person who is going through a difficult time, or to help a shut-in. Maybe God is asking you to do something even more radical, like volunteer at the prison or go speak with someone who needs your forgiveness or your apology. Any of these things could strike fear into the hearts of those God has called out of their comfort zone. The issue is this: if you know God has asked you to do or say something and you don't know why, you have a choice. You can:

1. Listen to what He's asking of you and then do it.
2. Seek further confirmation and, once received, do it.
3. Hear Him and ignore Him *or* run from Him (didn't work for Jonah, so it likely won't work for you).
4. Put yourself in a position that makes it difficult for God to speak to you. This can be accomplished by separating yourself from Him either through unbelief, sin, disobedience, or a lack of knowledge, understanding, or faith. Ultimately, you ignore Him and His request, or even potential requests, of you.

Reflections

Can you think of a time when you were at a crossroad and the decision you made changed the trajectory of your life for the positive?

Does God operate the same today as in the Bible?

Was there a time when your perception of faith was challenged?

TWO
Discovering Faith

SACRIFICE

Jesus was remarkable in so many ways, but what truly blows me away is that although He was the Son of God, He was also the Son of man, having the same emotions and temptations as the rest of us.

> He not only *knew* but had to *live* with the fact
> that His entire sinless life and existence would end in a
> horrible, painful, unjust death by crucifixion.
> He had to live with the knowledge that
> He would visit Hell!

I can't even comprehend what it would be like to live with this sort of knowledge and still go on with life. Although we may find it frustrating, the times when we're *not* able to see is likely because God knows it's best. After all, if it was good enough for those great men and women of faith who have gone before us, then it should be good enough for us.

Would Moses have embarked on his forty-year journey had he known all that he would endure? I somehow doubt that many of us would have jumped to the front of the queue, hoping for this assignment. And yet although the trials he faced were agonizing, he also witnessed miracle after miracle firsthand. He spoke with God, and God spoke with Him, unlike any other. He was on the roller coaster before any such invention had been manufactured! The highs were high, and the lows were low.

I've also learned that what may appear to us as obedient and sacrificial actions on our part is ultimately still about God providing us with a gift. When doing "our part" and things get difficult, it's tempting to pout and remind God of all that we've done for Him. Yet in the end, it's about God choosing to bless us.

> When opportunities arise to "give until it hurts,"
> we are provided with the chance to prove our faith.

This not only pleases Him but, in the end, blesses us! We still win! It's a gift. Others have been used mightily by God, and we can be too. It has nothing to do with what we've done for Him and everything to do with what He's done for us, knowing that in the end, without faith it is *impossible* to please Him.

If you find this thinking to be confusing or foreign to you, I implore you to sit down and have a conversation with God. Ask Him to open your eyes, ears, and heart to His perspective. Ask Him to reveal Himself and His ways to you in a manner in which you will know without a shadow of a doubt that you have heard and understood.

For those who are deeper in this walk and are still grappling with "faith," you'll likely need to re-examine your beliefs. Lay aside worldly or religious views and immerse yourself in God's. Perhaps somewhere along the way you received incorrect teaching or simply misunderstood a lesson. Ask God to help you to learn and receive His truths. It's important that you know you're not alone. It's because there are so many who don't understand faith that I was motivated to share my story.

> When Jesus said to His disciples "Follow me,"
> they didn't know where they were going
> or what they would be doing.
> They simply went!

When Moses wandered through the desert, he was unaware of the challenges he'd face, let alone the destination or how long it would take to get there. By faith, Abraham laid his beloved son Isaac on the altar when asked. By faith, the walls of Jericho fell down, and because of faith, kingdoms were subdued and folks were raised from the dead. Now that's pretty incredible stuff! I definitely want to be a part of these kinds of adventures. To do so, however, means refusing to allow misunderstandings or fear to stand in the way. We must be continually available, seeking after Him with a willingness to "act" when called.

I could feel the presence of the Lord in a way unlike any other. It was as though I'd been transported to another place and time. My heart was bursting as I worshipped with complete abandon, captivated by His love, declaring His truths with a confidence and boldness like never before.

I wasn't in a church but in a prison. We were leading a number of incarcerated youth in a time of passionate, vulnerable, honest, transparent worship. It was one of the first times I could ever recall being completely unencumbered by formality and religious expectations. I was anointed with a freedom to sing and speak of God's goodness in a way unlike any other. Surely this was heaven and not prison!

I was taken back to reality as I recalled an earlier comment from one of the younger band members, who jokingly inferred that these teens wouldn't be able to relate to someone my age. Insecurity bubbled to the surface, and I began to believe the "lie." Not many minutes later, though, a number of these same teens rose to their feet, making commitments to follow Christ. I was overwhelmed and unable to conceal my joy. I erupted with, "I'm so proud of you!" It was out of my mouth before I could stop it. I realized what a "mom" thing it had been to say.

As I internally reprimanded myself, the Lord whispered into my ear, "That's the first time many of these boys have heard that." I was greatly comforted and could see He was using me, uniquely, and that each of us has a role to play. My focus needed to remain on Him and His plans, not the thoughtless words of others.

FEAR, FAITH, AND LOVE

Fear can greatly hinder us in our walk with God. Many don't realize that faith requires courage, and courage is not the absence of fear, just the ability to control it. Think of it this way:

> The definition of faith is essentially
> the same as the definition of fear.

When we live in fear, we believe that something we can't see (but fear) is going to happen. When we live by faith, we believe something we can't see (but hope for) is going to happen. Fear and faith have the same definition, but they come from very different sources. They also both find a way of coming to fruition. Wherever our focus lies, and on whatever our eyes are fixed, usually dictates what comes out of our mouths and eventually what becomes of our lives. It's far better to hope and have faith for that which is good than to live in fear over that which is evil. We need to keep our focus on Jesus.

It can get complicated, though, because we're also instructed to fear the Lord. This, however, is a healthy fear. "*The fear of the Lord is the beginning of wisdom*" (Psalm 111:10; see also Proverbs 9:10). The fear of the Lord brings knowledge (Proverbs 1:7); confidence, safety, and protection (Proverbs 14:26–27); riches, honour, and life (Proverbs 22:4); and longer life (Proverbs 10:27). Those who fear Him are watched over by Him (Psalm 33:18). In fearing the Lord, we realize that our very salvation is wrapped up in His judgment of us, of how He sees us. If we don't fear Him, then there's a chance we may not know Him as the Sovereign I AM. There's a chance we are living according to our ways and not His.

> If we don't fear the Lord, we might be relying on our
> own strength, and that's pride.

It's startling to note that pride (excessive self-esteem, conceit) is a dangerous sin, because when in this mindset, we don't see ourselves as needing the God of the universe. We don't realize that within the blink of an eye, our lives could be over, because in actual fact, everything is *not* within our control: "*Pride goes before destruction, and a haughty spirit before a fall*" (Proverbs 16:18). Pride sets us apart from God by lodging a nasty wedge between us and Him. God desires that nothing would separate us from His love. Even so, He has provided us with the freedom to make choices. He wants us to know Him because we *want* to know and serve Him. When encased in pride, we make it difficult for Him to pierce the thick covering we have wrapped around ourselves. This is not a good place to be, because when in this position, we don't have a teachable spirit. We think we either know it all or have it all. Of course, one earthquake, a massive heart attack, or an economic crisis, and that theory is quickly obliterated.

So rather than waiting for a tragedy, the solution is quite simple. We just need to open our hearts to the one who created us and allow His Son, our Saviour, into those parts of us that are resistant to Him so that He can love us, teach us, and heal us. We need to seek His face, knowing and trusting that bit by bit, day by day, our hearts will be softened and our faith will grow.

I've noticed that some denominations focus on revering God and His sovereignty, while others emphasize Jesus as friend. Both are correct, but on one hand, there's a chance that in being overly familiar and casual, we could potentially diminish His magnificence, while the other perspective could cause us to view Him as distant and out of reach. While it's true that our Lord is loving and forgiving, He's also a just and righteous judge, and as the Great I AM, deserves our love, respect, admiration, reverence, and obedience.

How can we both love and fear the Lord?

Allow me to share some compelling revelation. If we fear the Lord, then we care about what He thinks and what He says. We love Him, and we love His ways. We're focused on Him, on listening to Him, and on pleasing Him. If we fear people and care more about what they think than what God is saying, then we've chosen to love people above loving our Lord. We've chosen their way and not His. Even if we fear something evil or demonic, we have inadvertently given it power over us. We need to give all the love, power, and focus to our Lord and Saviour. We need to concentrate on God. If we take our eyes off God and instead set our gaze on a person, an organization, or the government, we allow their input to take priority. We express adoration toward them, ultimately giving them authority to reign in our hearts and minds. In essence, we say that the person or organization is correct, and God is wrong. Whoa, that's a heavy, but it is truth.

Conquering this may sound quite easy, but in reality, it can be a difficult process, especially for those who are given to people-pleasing. I know a little about this because, although not an extreme victim of this group, I did need to triumph over this issue and still struggle with it from time to time. I started the healing process by way of a *lot* of pain and rejection. I needed to overcome caring about the way I was perceived or judged while still caring for the people who were rejecting me. This is an entirely different subject, so I won't digress. Suffice to say, though, getting past pleasing, fearing, or loving people brought freedom, but it also required discipline. We need to have God's heart and be wholly surrendered to His ways.

> In scripture, when fear is mentioned in association with the Lord, it's coupled with love and reverence. Fear outside of the Lord is connected to anguish.

In scripture, when fear is mentioned in association with the Lord, it's coupled with love and reverence. Fear outside of the Lord is connected to anguish.

First John 4:18a says, "*There is no fear in love; but perfect love casts out fear, because fear involves torment …*"

Some people might feel this is simply too much to attain and that they will never "get there." Others might feel a little boastful, especially those who have heard, listened, and acted on promptings from the Holy Spirit. Let me just say that not even our faith is about us! Although people who live by faith might be admired, they must not be elevated to a place of awe. Yes, work and discipline are required, but even our faith comes from above.

Jesus is the author and finisher of our faith, so He receives all the honour and glory. I am well aware of how imperfect I am, of all the renovations that took place (and those that still must occur) in my life to bring me to a place of faith that is pleasing to the King. I'd be in great error and sin to take any credit for what I have learned or experienced. It is God! He is the one who transforms lives. All glory belongs to Him.

THE CALL

Living a fully-surrendered *adventure* in faith became my reality when, sometime around May 1997, I heard a sermon urging us to submit ourselves and our wills completely to God and to all that He would have us be and do. This may not sound very significant, especially considering that I had given my life to Christ a few days before my twelfth birthday, and by the time I'd reached twenty-eight, I had a pretty decent grasp of Lordship Salvation. So to finally get the idea of *complete* submission in my late thirties seemed a little delayed but also a little over the edge! I had always seen myself as a light in the world, living as Christ would have me live in my everyday world. I'd never really considered giving up *complete* control. After all, God was in authority over my life, but wasn't it up to me to run it? Of course it was!

Wrong! That day when I decided to give over complete control was the beginning of the ride of a lifetime, up and down and all around—like that roller coaster, yet from here on out, always in the grip of the Father's gentle, loving, protecting, and—let's not forget—refining hands, always moulding, always shaping.

Within days of making this commitment, I heard the voice of God. I really heard Him and *knew* He was speaking to me. This was powerful, because I'd experienced more than one miracle in my lifetime, but this was different. He said seven simple words that changed my life:

"I want *My* music in the world."

There was no more and no less. I shared it with my husband, Kevin, but otherwise kept it to myself, mulling it over in my head until finally one day I got up the courage to share it with a believer from work. After getting up the nerve to tell my co-worker what I thought I'd heard, I expected, maybe even hoped, that she'd tell me I had lost my mind. But instead, what I got was an emphatic, "*Yes, this is right!*"

Four years earlier she had attended a session given by a man of God who had received three consecutive dreams from the Lord. The dreams were about how God was going to use His music to reach hearts and souls for Jesus. She promised to bring the details of the prophetic word the following day. As I listened to her speak and as she shared the power of this word from God, I knew without a shadow of a doubt I was called to this (see Appendix I). God was fully in control now, and He had a job for little ol' me! It astounded me that the one person with whom I'd shared these words would turn out to be the unlikely vessel He'd use to confirm the call.

I sat out on my deck, basking in the warmth of this beautiful sunny day, listening intently to the recordings given me by my co-worker. James Ryle related his three dreams, known as the "Sons of Thunder" prophecy. The crackling and poor quality of the tape faded into the background of a message and a word that resonated with every fibre of my being. I was riveted by his message, as previously unarticulated words from my own heart had been given a voice. His words evoked a passion and conviction within me that I'd never previously experienced.

He described how godly producers, musicians, and singers, previously "hidden," were soon going to be used for the Lord's purposes to touch the hearts and minds of those who didn't know Him. He spoke of the power of God in music, the treasured inheritances being wrongfully spent on ourselves rather than shared with the world, and how evangelistic musicians would travel (with freedom and easily mobile, like motorcyclists) to places and by means that others wouldn't and couldn't. He spoke of God releasing anointed worshipping warriors into the streets.

Yes! I was one of these. I knew it and was struck by the overwhelming realization that this was my purpose, my destiny, and my call. My heart was racing. My soul had been dramatically awakened, and I knew that my life would never again be the same.

I got into the Word and sought God in prayer. This was real! I didn't know why He had called me, only that He had called me. Sure, I'd been involved in music throughout my entire life, but I didn't know anything about *His* music. I had a wide range of experience in the secular music industry—you know, being a light. But *how* exactly was I supposed to bring His music to the world? What exactly was *His* music? Who would perform? Where would they perform? Who would attend? Who would support such an endeavour? The only thing I knew for certain was that it had to be done with excellence and integrity.

There was much to be done, and although there were more questions than answers, I forged ahead, led by God. At least my background consisted of having worked for years as a singer, actor, and also as a professional marketing and promotions manager in the arts. This would be my starting point. I prayed and sought out experts, some of whom I already knew, and some of whom I would need to meet for the first time. I was off and running, all the while continuing on with my full-time job in communications within the government.

Finally, after considering, pursuing, and eventually finding no real understanding, support, or unity from within the current framework of the church, I felt the best way to move forward was to venture out and produce the concerts myself under an already established business—one I had initiated a few years prior. I was fully aware of what a massive undertaking it would be, but I had run out of partnership options and was compelled to obey the call. I was starting from scratch with everything—naming it appropriately, developing an audience, soliciting corporate sponsorship, finding volunteers, and deciding what "it" would be. At long last, "it" was birthed—a series of Christian concerts to take place in a number of professional venues of varying sizes throughout the city. Prior to this time, Christian concerts had usually taken place in churches, and attendees generally belonged to the host church.

> I was resolute in my decision to be completely inclusive,
> ensuring that absolutely every person—churched,
> un-churched, believers, non-believers, young, and old—
> would feel comfortable and welcome
> and not threatened in any way.

For this reason, I decided to book mainstream halls exclusively. Of course, this would significantly increase my costs, but I couldn't fathom doing it any other way. Nearly everything was in place! It was exciting and frightening all at the same time.

After approximately five months of preparation, the labour had intensified, and I was running on empty. I requested that my full-time government position hours be cut down and, against all logic and governing rules, it was granted me! This was the favour of the Lord. Still, I knew another huge step of faith was upon us.

We needed to sell our home before we could proceed.

Without the "stability" associated with a full-time job (and with my husband being a self-employed musician), it was imperative that we be free from debt. The sale of our home didn't mean we would be particularly liquid, but at least the burden of debt would be lifted. We looked for an appropriate home to rent, and God provided. As a matter of fact, He provided a home twice the size of the one released and one large enough to give the company an office. Up until this time, I had worked in the primary bedroom of our tiny duplex. This was another gift from God, and we were ecstatic!

Our steps of faith were clearly being blessed, giving us the courage and fortitude to move forward. I was entering unfamiliar territory not only as a producer but also as a promoter. I was just one of two professional gospel music promoters in all of Canada and, lonely or not, prepared or not, January 23, 1998 marked our very first performance.

There were many incredible moments to celebrate as a result of this premier event, yet I struggled with disappointment over the size of the crowd. In faith, I had anticipated that we'd have a full house. We did have a good-sized crowd, but it wasn't a full house. I hadn't counted on this. I became fixated on the potential loss in revenue. It was the beginning of a very steep and often painful learning curve for me. What did become apparent was that the show itself was just one piece of the plan.

This was never more evident than when I tried, in my own strength, to garner media attention to promote the concerts. It's important to note here that media relations had been my world for the previous decade. For this reason, I had mistakenly relied upon my own expertise! Imagine my surprise when there were *no* responses from the media to cover the concerts! Horrified and humbled, I got on my knees, and *while* praying, the phone rang. It was the largest newspaper in the city calling to arrange an interview! Then … the media floodgates opened!

The artist appearing in my first concert was Sherman Andrus, an icon, a Grammy winner, a friend to Elvis Presley. While doing a taped interview at a local radio station, another host was so enthused to discover he was in the building that he "sent" for him and requested that he do a live interview as soon as he finished the first one. He agreed.

As I glanced at the clock on the wall, I realized we'd been at the radio station longer than anticipated. I dashed outside to pop more money into the parking meter, hoping I would beat the attendant there and avoid getting a ticket. I made it! With a sigh of relief, I strolled back to the studio.

As I re-entered the building, I noticed something had changed. Even though it had only been a few minutes, the atmosphere was different. The receptionist at the front desk had tears in her eyes, and the music that was playing wasn't the usual fare. It was a song of declaration, and it was captivating the attention of all who were in the building. Then it hit me: it was my artist. He was singing an impromptu, hauntingly beautiful, a cappella version of "His Eye Is on the Sparrow."

I worked my way back to the studio, compelled by the faces I saw along the way. Most had stopped working and were just standing still, as though frozen, quietly listening to him sing. It was stunning. With all the planning in the world, I couldn't have orchestrated anything so wonderful. It was amazing and anointed, and it was God!

A similar moment occurred when after an interview on a popular morning television show, the host was so taken by this artist that he asked him to come back the following morning to co-host the entire show! The next day was Robbie Burns Day, and just as they were about to dig into the haggis, the host abruptly stopped to ask our artist if he'd like to say grace. Naturally, he did, and hopefully so did thousands of viewers!

> I was astonished by how God was using the mainstream media to accomplish His purposes.

His music was in the world, in a professional venue, but also in print, on radio, and on television. Who'd have thought? Maybe only a few hundred were at the event, but thousands were being introduced to Him through the media. God was using the mainstream press more powerfully and creatively than I could have ever imagined. Thank God that He is the one in control!

Just one month after the first show, we mounted our second. This time I really went out on a limb by producing the event in a well-known local hot spot, a night club that was known for drawing world-class musicians. This decision to bring His music to the people—all people—was in direct response to the great commission to "*Go into all the world*" (Mark 16:15). I felt strongly that it was in keeping with how Jesus would have done things, and that was good enough for me! So despite a few raised eyebrows from the more "religious" faction about the choice of venue, which by the way turned out to be brilliant, it was an outstanding evening.

A great deal happened as a result of this concert, not least of which was the beginning of some lifelong friendships between me and a couple of the singers. The house band, of which my husband was a member, began to grow in popularity, and it was evident that this gifted group was a key ingredient to the success of these shows. A strong band full of professional, Christian, anointed players, all of whom were homegrown, was a huge plus!

The employees at the bar were moved beyond belief, as were the many in attendance who didn't belong to a church family. We were gaining positive recognition from the community and the media. They loved our first two events, and trust was building. Fear was being alleviated, and the world was beginning to see the sincerity of our hearts. But amidst the blessings, a storm was brewing. The immensity of this responsibility, combined with ongoing negative undercurrents, was daunting.

We were experiencing spiritual attack like never before.

I was being hit hard with everything—illness, conflict, oppression, relational difficulties, and jealous accusations from church leaders (the majority of whom I didn't know). My husband and I were met with the harsh reality that we had stepped onto a battlefield. This had somehow been lost on me prior to this time. As the season of concerts continued, the learning continued.

Working with immigration, Revenue Canada, the IRS, and Nashville's talent agents and management companies was an education in itself. I found it staggering that many groups chose to sing with instrumental tracks rather than with our very professional band! I felt sure that once they heard the rave reviews from those who had worked with our musicians and knew of their outstanding capabilities, they would change their minds, but sadly, this wasn't realized until much later.

I was very uncomfortable with this "trend," because my goal wasn't to be just as good as the shows in the world but better, and tracks would be completely unacceptable in the world. Why was it acceptable in the Christian world? I was baffled but needed to proceed as best as I could. What this did accomplish, however, was to motivate me to shift my focus onto some of the outstanding *local* talent, who I knew would *love* the opportunity to work with this band. It would give them an occasion to use their gifts, garner some attention, and hopefully add momentum to their music careers.

As a result, two of the shows from that season ended up featuring local artists. Not only did this tie in with my current focus, but it also brought to fruition an old dream. When I originally started the company, the concept was to provide a platform for both promising and established artists. I wanted to give them an opportunity to be professionally marketed and promoted in performances designed to showcase their talent. At that time, I had no idea it would be Christian music. Now, five years later, here it was. The stage was set, and I was delighted by the incredible response. The live music venue was bursting at the seams, filled to more than twice its capacity! This was even better than the soft-seat theatre.

A group of fifty accountants had booked their table early on. Every year, they would congregate at this club to celebrate the end of tax season. Initially, they were disgruntled when they found out the evening would feature gospel music, but the nightclub staff encouraged them to stay! And stay they did—all evening—and had a tremendous time, hooting and clapping throughout the entire show. They genuinely enjoyed the music, and we enjoyed the freshness of their enthusiasm.

It's encouraging to note that throughout this inaugural season of concerts, people were making decisions to follow Christ! Believe it or not, this actually bothered many of the church leaders. Go figure. In spite of the opposition, I was beginning to get a handle on what was expected of me but was weighed down by the associated responsibility, my incredibly busy schedule, and battling a health scare of my own. I just kept pushing through the difficulties

Between the concerts, my job, my church, my health, and my family, I was juggling a lot of balls. Something had to change before I dropped one.

> It was time for another leap of faith, a decision to completely leave my "stable" job, which also meant forfeiting all remaining "security."

This was extraordinarily difficult, given that, although not in debt, we didn't have anything extra with which to operate. We would be fully dependent on God and on this new venture. We were primed and ready for season two. With no regular income, this meant increased pressure and some penniless and lonely times. Pioneering was more challenging than either of us had ever foreseen.

Reflections

Have you ever received/heard a word or a prophecy that was life-changing? How did you respond?

Can you identify specific fears you may have that hinder obedience?

Is there anything you've had to give up/surrender to be obedient?

THREE

Holding on to Faith

IN THE WORLD

There were just two-and-a-half months to prepare for the next season, and it was grander than the first. I produced a total of ten concerts! One of the concerts was in two cities, and four of the groups were from Nashville. In keeping with my commitment to local talent, each of the headliners had a local opening act. As expected, there were plenty of ups and downs throughout the season. I was growing deeper in my faith while also battling discouragement.

One of the more significant and unique things that happened was that, despite the trepidation of a few critics, I decided to do something quite bold and hire a scaled-down version of the local professional symphony orchestra and incorporate a two-hundred-voice choir into a very significant gala event that featured the best jazz vocal group on the planet, Take 6.

Needless to say, this attracted a lot of attention. In fact, there was so much attention, mostly positive but some controversial, that the large concert hall was filled almost to capacity for two performances. Incredibly, more than half of the audience came as a result of mainstream marketing! Also significant is how God used the event to provide a witness to many of the orchestral musicians and choir members on stage, those who were actually performing in the concert! Isn't that just like our loving, tender-hearted Father, to ensure that many of those who wouldn't have attended on their own were actually paid to be there and hear the gospel?

> We were in the world but not of it, and we were starting to get the hang of what it was to take the "salt and light"

concept to a new level, one that involved a bolder stance, and it was rewarding.

It was also fascinating that God was using us, a non-church group, to bring healing to the body. As we incorporated folks from various churches and organizations into these events, harmony was established. It wasn't unusual for forty or fifty churches to be represented at any given concert, and that was just on stage. God was at work, and the walls of resentment, hurt, and indifference were coming down.

A truly memorable moment in season two took place at the final concert. In sharp contrast to the previous gala, which was big and majestic, this event was quiet, introspective, and intimate in nature.

A sea of people surrounded me as I stood in the lobby of the theatre after a beautiful concert featuring Australia's Michelle Tumes. An unexpected tug at my arm drew my attention away from the merchandise table as a friend frantically summoned me into the theatre.

I attempted to glean a better understanding as to the urgency of her request, but as I rushed behind her through the crowd, all I heard was, "Something is happening." I had no idea what was going on, but when I entered the theatre, it was as though a glow permeated the room.

A young man was on his knees, arms raised, sobbing uncontrollably while friends stood around him, praying. As I approached, he came to his feet, staggered over to me, hugged me, and said, "Thank you for doing this. Thank you for what you do." This un-churched young man had been so touched by the music and the Spirit of the living God that at the end of the concert, with no prompting by the artist and no altar call, he had asked the Lord to reveal Himself to him. He wanted to know God for himself, not simply through those who had invited him. The next thing he knew, he was on his knees, and Jesus was in front of him!

I couldn't get over the fact that this brand-new believer had already fully grasped our hearts. He "got it." It was just as promised in the prophetic word. God was at work in and through the anointing of the music.

Having been immersed in music for most of my life, it was an easy transition to see that the anointed arts could be a powerful evangelism tool. Music and art have the unique ability to speak as a language of the spirit unlike any other. The arts are powerful in that they're able to reach out and touch people deep in their hearts before their heads have had a chance to "catch up" and analyze all that's going on.

It's extraordinary to see what can happen to the coldest and hardest of hearts when the Holy Spirit touches them through song, dance, or art. Although much discussion has ensued throughout churches world-wide over all things stylistically-related, generationally-related, and doctrinally-related, I would encourage folks to focus on that which is God-related. J.S. Bach said it perfectly with this statement: "The aim and final reason of all music should be nothing else but the glory of God and the refreshment of the spirit." That's it! It's not about hymns versus choruses, choirs versus bands, or the youth versus the seniors. It's about the spirit behind the music. It's about the spirit that's influencing the art.

> *"That which is born of the flesh is flesh, and that which is born of the Spirit is spirit."* (John 3:6)

While these concerts were ultimately about seeing the lost led to the Lord, they were also about seeing a forgotten group, which I refer to as "music evangelists," used in new and innovative ways. It's such an amazing witness to a non-believing musician or musician "wannabe" to hear some of the best players they've ever heard in a setting or environment in which it's clearly evident that these musical geniuses are Christians. What a testimony!

I've seen firsthand how powerful it is, and I've seen the lost drawn to Christ as a result. While I know we're expected to reach the poor, I'm also compelled to reach those who are poor in heart and spirit. Folks don't have to be poverty-stricken to need Jesus.

> The lost aren't just those suffering
> with addiction or homelessness.
> They're also the gifted and the affluent.

The lost are lost, regardless of income or position. People of influence also need Jesus, and when they decide to serve Him, they can take their passion and drive for excellence and use it to effect positive change for the Kingdom. With Christ in them, they'll live a life of even greater significance than before. People like this are integral to prompting real and lasting change in our world. These "influencers" must be reassured that when living for Christ, they don't need to take steps backward but that they should continue in achieving superior workmanship, promoting godly change in a world that needs the hope that comes from knowing Jesus.

People in the world are watching us, so we must maintain pure and clean hearts that are right with God, consistent and in line with His Word, and distinctly set apart in all we say and do. That's a tall order but a goal worth realizing. I've been blessed with the opportunity to work with some of the finest internationally-renowned mainstream artists out there, and I did it to the best of my ability. When turning my sights to His music, I never wanted to give God any less than I'd given to the rest, but rather more! It's an honour to serve Him and to do so skillfully and whole-heartedly.

With the third season of concerts, we experienced unbelievable financial hardships and were also blessed with unfathomable spiritual success. As I ruminated on where we'd been and where we were going, I was reminded of the purpose behind this effort.

> We were here to bring God's Word,
> through music, to the lost, to the hurting,
> to those who didn't know Him. This was the goal.

I had to keep this my focus. I could see what God was doing with me spiritually. I had changed. It wasn't enough to put on a great outreach show. I *really* wanted to see the lost saved. My desire to be in the will of God was overshadowing my need to balance the books.

God was asking me to bring even more to the table "'til it hurt," which it did. I needed to trust Him completely, which I was attempting to do but was not always successful in achieving. He wanted me to see what was happening on a spiritual level. He was giving me words of knowledge and wisdom, visions and strange new gifts. I guess it's not surprising that the closer I grew to Him, the further some of my friends seemed to be from me. It was a confusing and difficult time as I waded through and processed all that was happening to me.

It was also time to ask myself some pointed questions. How many non-believing people were attending the concerts on their own initiative? How many could afford these events? How many were actually being invited by believers, which had been our original hope? Although we'd seen great success, I knew God wanted more. If they weren't coming to us, then we needed to go to them, to the highways and byways! After all, this entire initiative was about the lost, so we had to ensure that they were reached.

We began a phone blitz for that entire season, inviting people from the inner city, various missions, pregnancy counselling centres, women's shelters, and the like, determined to give away at least 10 per cent of our seats, and what happened next was astounding. They arrived … in droves! Hundreds of non-believers attended concerts in two major Canadian cities over that season. It was astonishing to see how moved they were—not just by the music or that we cared enough to invite them—but because of the work of the Holy Spirit.

At our first event of the third season, there was one woman who had not shown emotion in ten years who experienced incredible breakthrough. One of the workers from a pregnancy counselling centre testified that one of their young clients had decided *not* to abort her unborn child, scheduled for the following day! One of my more dedicated volunteers was greatly moved by an elderly homeless man who had never been to an event like this before. He had done his utmost to dress up for the occasion, and although his jacket was worn and wrinkled, his face shone.

> There was healing, saved souls, and saved lives.
> God's will was being accomplished. What a ride!
> This was most assuredly worth all the pain.

The spiritual activity was inspiring, but we were greatly disheartened by the amount of money we were losing. So often I had heard the phrase "God's will. God's bill." So why were we struggling?

I was in the midst of running errands a couple of days prior to the next concert when I had a truly astounding vision. Strangely, the entire thing happened while I was driving.

In the vision, I could see myself sitting at a table with a huge pile of money in front of me. I was guarding it, protecting it, watching over it. As I sat there, I could hear the most horrendous, blood-curdling screams I'd ever heard. I looked over and saw a person literally being sucked in by huge flames. It was a horrific fire, and the terror that ran through my soul was almost more than I could bear. It was truly frightening!

For a brief moment in the vision, I had thought to myself: "If I leave to go help, then the money will surely be taken, but if I don't leave, the people will most definitely die." I jumped up and ran over to pull them out of the fire. When I returned, the money was gone. That was the end of the vision. My heart was racing and my body was shaking as I pulled over to the side of the road.

This was clearly a word from the Lord.

> I knew my financial woes were nothing, not a concern.
> I needed to focus my energies on allowing God to use me
> so that, regardless of the cost, people might be saved.

I had an even deeper understanding of the devastation associated with being separated from God. I also knew we should be sharing Jesus more, praying for the lost, and wholeheartedly believing for miracles.

> People need Jesus. Someone needed to tell them about Jesus. Someone needed to decide that they were more concerned with seeing souls set free than with their own potential rejection or personal loss.

When the next group to perform arrived, we discussed the whole idea of an altar call, something I had previously veered away from. I told them how God had spoken to me, and I said they should do whatever they felt led to do.

Well, let me just say, of the hundreds of people we gave tickets to, most stood up and gave their lives to Christ those nights! One particularly touching image that's engraved in my memory is the sight of an entire family standing together at their seats, hand in hand, weeping, as they committed to live out their days for Christ. I was seeing something I hadn't seen before on this scale. People wanted to be saved. They wanted freedom. This was miraculous. This was significant. This was the purpose. It was all coming together, and although there were hardships, God was with us.

As I prayed for direction in relation to our fourth season, He made it clear we were to stop. We were not to continue down the same path but needed to pause and await further instruction on "the plan." In retrospect, I think what happened here was not so much about refining "the plan" but rather refining me.

My walk at this point had been more of a sprint, and I realize now that God wanted me to slow down. At the time it was devastating, because we were on a roll, and now He was asking us to stop. Rather than seeing it as a gift, I saw it as punishment. It made no sense to me until much later. Sure, I had made some blunders along the way, so it was easy to believe God was upset with me. Others fed into this mindset, which only added to my deep sorrow. Of course, once my thinking cleared, I knew that in Christ there is therefore now no condemnation. Although He may correct us, it's not because He's angry with us but because He loves us.

Along with refinement, He was seeing to it that I grew in my knowledge of the Word, that I rested and re-gained my health. I was obedient but also terribly frustrated—feeling stuck but hearing His voice well enough to know I was right where I was supposed to be. There was spiritual growth and continued confirmation that God would use music to reach souls, and that was encouraging. I had lived in the miraculous, and I couldn't imagine going back to the way life had been before the call. The painful lesson learned here was

> I was here for God and His purposes
> and not the other way around.

If I needed to rest for a season, then so be it. If it was time to pause and reflect, then it was time to pause and reflect, regardless of my thoughts and feelings on the subject. God is so patient. Even though we can revert to behaving like self-absorbed, impatient two-year-olds wanting what we want, the way we want it, when we want it, how we want it, He remains loving and long-suffering toward us!

In the end, although stubborn as a mule, I did release the ministry, knowing all too well that it was His ministry and not mine, His will and not mine.

HIS WILL

So what is God's will? I've heard it said that the only way to make certain we're in the centre of God's perfect will for our lives is to go to the centre of God's perfect Word. The verse that's right in the centre of the Bible is Psalm 118:8: "*It is better to trust in the Lord than to put confidence in man.*"

This is also what Paul speaks of in Romans 12:2, when he says, "*And do not be conformed to this world, but be transformed by the renewing of your mind, that you may prove what is that good and acceptable and perfect will of God.*" This doesn't happen overnight, although with God all things are possible.

> This happens when we allow Him, day by day,
> to re-train our minds so that, over time,
> we think more like God than like the world.

The more input we receive from the world, the more we think like the world, and the more we become like the world. However, the more we immerse ourselves in God, the more we become like God.

When Jesus taught us to pray, He used the words, "*Your will be done on earth as it is in heaven*" (Matthew 6:10b). This tells me that God wants us to live here on earth according to His way, the way in which we'd picture life in heaven. Having not been there myself, I presume this means living a life filled with love, hope, peace, and joy, esteeming others above ourselves, ever and always worshipping our King, exalting the name of Jesus with reckless abandon, fully engaged in an intimate relationship with Him.

The best way to do this is to make a concerted effort toward learning how God operates, how He thinks, His perspective. We have to grab hold of what's important to Him, which inevitably will be completely contrary to the way of the world, or the way we've likely been taught. As we do this and grow closer to Him, the specifics of our roles will be revealed to us.

We should also become aware of the strengths, gifts, talents, and passions He has placed within us, paying particular attention to the environments and situations in which we excel. Once we've done our part by developing our skills and serving in obedience, and we think we've sorted it all out, we mustn't be surprised when God stretches us into areas we hadn't originally considered. He's like that!

> He'll rarely ask us to do something
> we could do without Him.

So in pushing us and stretching us, He's sure to keep us close, because we know full well that we're unable to do what He's asked of us in our own strength. Once we realize how desperately we need Him in order to accomplish an assigned task, then we're in a good place. It's also crucial that we develop a more intimate walk with the Holy Spirit. He's the one Jesus sent to guide and counsel us, so His role is hugely significant to walking in power!

As we learn to hear His voice, we'll grow in our understanding of the will God has for our lives. Because each person and situation are unique, it's nearly impossible to determine what will happen and in what order, so try to view it as an ongoing process. If at first you can't seem to hear His voice, then spend more quiet time with Him; read the Word, pray, and also say nothing at all. Invite the Holy Spirit to speak to you and minister to you, being solely attuned to Him. Permit yourself the time to just soak Him in. You may not hear anything right away, but I'm confident that over time, you will. After all, we reap that which we sow. This is a biblical principle, and God keeps His word. So even if in the beginning it's just a faint, small, still voice, or perhaps a prompting or urging that comes by way of the Holy Spirit, keep listening, believing in faith that you will perceive what the Lord is saying.

You may begin to sense that something is being said or asked of you and then mistakenly attribute it to the cheese pizza you ate the evening prior! Don't be too quick to dismiss these things. Talk to God and ask for confirmation and clarification. Over time, you'll find that your "hearing" is improving and that day by day, step by step, you're moving into your purpose. Of course it needs to be said that only Moses got a burning bush. Some receive dreams, some visions, some hear audibly, while others get a powerful sense. How and when He speaks is as unique as we are and as creative as He is.

I must go back once again to the bigger picture in association with His will, because Jesus also said *"And this is the will of Him who sent Me, that everyone who sees the Son and believes in Him may have everlasting life; and I will raise him up at the last day"* (John 6:40).

In the end, in order to be in His will, we must believe.

We must have faith. It seems simple. It's an easy concept, so why has it become so difficult and complicated? I think it's because of all that we're up against. Have you ever wondered why so much effort and energy have gone into attempts to disprove and discredit Jesus? Why is there very little blasphemy going on when it comes to Mohammed, Allah, Buddha, or Joseph Smith?

It's because the only one that concerns the enemy is Jesus.

The devil knows Jesus is the only road to God and to eternal life with Him. Jesus is the way, the truth, and the life. He's the only one who threatens the devil in his quest for souls. He's the only one Satan must deter folks from following. Don't be deceived! Think about it. Pray about it. The will of God is that you believe in Jesus, that you have faith in Him, and this faith will save you.

> *Preach the word! Be ready in season and out of season. Convince, rebuke, exhort, with all longsuffering and teaching. For the time will come when they will not endure sound doctrine, but according to their own desires, because they have itching ears, they will heap up for themselves teachers; and they will turn their ears away from the truth, and be turned aside to fables.* (2 Timothy 4:2–4)

We see people being misled all the time. How sad when people start to trust talk show hosts, biased journalists, and bloggers or social media influencers above our Heavenly Father. We must be strong and of good courage. If initially the assignments God gives appear small and seemingly unimportant, they're not. If they matter to Him, they should matter to us.

HIS WORD

One of the most important things I've learned and tend to repeat is that in order to truly understand what the reality of living by faith looks like, one must get into the Word of God. A gap needs to be bridged between those who are living by faith, those who have faith (but think that some of us have simply taken it too far), and those who really don't understand the faith journey at all. It is here that I am hoping to shed a little light on how to get faith.

As we dig into what the scriptures have to say, we're met with our first significant stumbling block to moving forward. This may sound blunt, but I've found that many who question or criticize this walk don't actually read their Bibles, and those who do frequently don't have a revelation of the scriptures that comes by way of Holy Spirit understanding. This is where things can get messy, because it has the potential to sound judgmental, which is not intended. What I'm trying to say is that the basis of my faith comes from the Word of God. While many call themselves Christians, not all are personally familiar with what the Bible says. Reading the Bible brings knowledge, and when the Holy Spirit gets involved, revelation increases, as does understanding: *"So then faith comes by hearing, and hearing by the word of God"* (Romans 10:17).

> This means that the only way to get faith is to know God, and the primary way to know God is through His Word and the Holy Spirit.

Because we're also encouraged to seek godly counsel, we need to make certain that the people who are speaking into our lives are absolutely offering us godly advice or insight. We should know our advisors are in the Word and that they're hearing from God. We must make certain that what they're saying to us lines up with scripture, which means that we must know scripture:

> *Blessed is the man who walks not in the counsel of the ungodly, nor stands in the path of sinners, nor sits in the seat of the scornful; but his delight is in the law of the Lord, and in His law he meditates day and night.* (Psalm 1:1–2)

> If you don't know what the Word of God says, it will be exceedingly difficult for you to know if the advice you are receiving or the preaching you are hearing is from the Lord.

I once heard a sermon by a greatly respected preacher in which he asked a very challenging question. It went something like, "Yes, you believe in Jesus Christ, but are you a *follower* of Jesus Christ?" There *is* a difference. We need to learn His Word, His teachings, His ways, and His voice for ourselves. If our only education is by way of other people, it can prove dangerous, because even preachers and teachers can be off-track. You'll never know if you're receiving false teaching if you're not familiar with the truth. It's all a process and a journey, one step at a time. Still, you need to actually take those steps. So I encourage you to get into the Word and get faith!

For those who have read the Bible, have you ever stopped to think about these people of faith, whose stories are told in scripture, as real people and not just fictional characters in a fairy tale? Have you thought about how they must have felt when asked by God to do seemingly outrageous things for Him? Have you considered the uniqueness of each of their stories? In other words, not program-oriented or constrained by tradition or culture but tailored by God to suit His plans and purposes, completely and uniquely ordained and designed by Him.

Have you read about and contemplated the faith of Daniel, Joshua, Abraham, Moses, Paul, John the Baptist, and Jesus' disciples? Have you read about what was asked of them and then really, really thought about it? Have you truly reflected on what it means to be called to live by faith?

Sometimes it's easy to imagine or believe that if we were the ones living in biblical times, we would have made the correct choices.

> Sometimes it's easy to imagine or believe that if we were the ones living in biblical times, we would have made the correct choices.

With that said, we have the distinct advantage of skipping on ahead to the end of each story to see how things turned out. We're able to easily identify the errors these folks made along the way because we can see the whole picture. They couldn't. Again, just like today, not everyone in biblical times was called to the same thing, but those who were called to live an extreme measure of faith had a difficult road to travel!

> Those who are called to live this sort of faith
> need support, not criticism.

What I've discovered as I read in God's Word about those who have gone before, whom God has called to live in ways completely foreign to those around them, is that after all these thousands of years, not much has changed! God still asks some people to do what looks completely crazy to the world and the church. There are still people who obey God. There are still people who are confused by the actions of the obedient, and those who mock. Same old, same old. If you want to understand what drives people of faith to do what they do, then you absolutely need to delve into the scriptures and try to put yourself in the shoes of the people used by God in this way in the past. Although it can be sad and even difficult to hear of the trauma, martyrdom, hardships, and pain endured, especially by those who lived faith-filled, obedient lives, it will bring increased understanding.

Let's take, for example, Job's life. One must really wonder why God allowed Satan to torment this man who had been consistently faithful and obedient. God not only allowed this adversity but was so confident in Job's faith that He encouraged Satan to try Job. Through it all, though, God's protection was on Job; He would not allow Satan to take his life. Job's friends all had theories about the reasons for these trials, and they were *all* wrong. There is a lesson in this!

Then there was David. Why did God love David with such fervency? David was far from perfect and had, in fact, committed some fairly significant sins, yet God had tremendous love for him. I think it's because David was passionate and real in his relationship with God. David was honest, transparent, humble, and openly confessed his sins when found to be in error.

> David's heart was true. His repentance was genuine.
> His worship was pure.

What about Noah? Here is someone we envision as a godly man, faithfully serving the Lord, who as a result of his faith was chosen and set apart to do something noteworthy. Although we might be inclined to focus on the end of that story, picturing how after so much toiling and labour, he and his family were ultimately saved from a deadly flood that completely destroyed the earth, there is so much more to this tale. Can you imagine how overwhelmed Noah and his family must have felt throughout this entire ordeal? For years Noah had suffered tremendous hardships as he endeavoured to do all that had been asked of him, likely appearing to his friends and critics as though he was either eccentric, insane, or both. Think about how incredibly tortured he was, bombarded by malicious remarks from those who watched him "waste" his days, weeks, months, years. There he was, out in the public eye, open to scrutiny 24/7, building an enormous structure meant to withstand a flood in a world that had never seen rain! I can almost hear the whispers, the mocking, and the jeers that must have haunted him. Worse yet would have been the horrific assault to his senses when death surrounded him on all sides as every corner of the earth was being ravaged by a catastrophic event unlike any other.

> Although safe inside the ark, Noah mustn't have felt particularly victorious as his friends and acquaintances were tragically dying all around him.

I'm confident he was grateful that God had spared his life and the lives of his immediate family, but I wonder at the horrors and atrocious memories of that event. I'm doubtful he felt triumphant amidst so much trauma, loss, and chaos. We see scaled-down versions of tragedy all the time and subsequently question how we've avoided certain death while another wasn't so blessed. Perhaps we're the ones who have lived the tragedy and we don't feel blessed at all. Either way, these are big issues, and often the answers don't come in this lifetime. We need to trust that the God of the universe knows exactly what He's doing and that He loves us with an everlasting love.

It was one of only a few intimate conversations I can ever recall having had with my aunt. She and my uncle, a pastor, had been missionaries in Venezuela for decades. Our times together were infrequent and therefore precious.

As we sat together during one of those rare occasions, I was struck by her candor as she spoke of her grandson, who at the age of nine had passed away. He'd suffered a major heart attack outside his school while waiting for the bus and died right there in front of his teachers and classmates.

My teenage head was finding it difficult to fathom that anything good could come from such a tragedy. I marvelled as she spoke of her undeniable peace and her gratitude to God for having shown mercy in taking this precious child when He had. She was certain that He had saved her grandson from something far worse that was to transpire in the future. She was happy to know that he was safe in his Heavenly Father's arms rather than to have seen him suffer something far more dreadful, or worse yet, turn from God as an adult, causing his family to wonder if, in the end, they'd see him in glory. This way, they knew!

Please hear me when I say that absolutely every situation is different, and God is doing a different work in each of us, so there is no formula or answer for why these things happen, only that they do. What I do know is that while there's much that we may not understand, we still need to come to a place of trusting that the same God who created us also loves us. There are times in this walk when we "give it our all" yet find ourselves greatly disappointed in the outcome. Walking by faith isn't easy.

Once we have come to terms with the fact that God's Word is truth and God's way is the only way, we're in a far better position to serve. When folks grumble about the associated challenges, I remind them that it's not about them.

> We have a very real responsibility to push past the obstacles for the sake of those who will follow.

We have children, grandchildren, and great grandchildren who are counting on us to leave them a rich spiritual heritage. Scripture emphasizes the significant impact of our actions, both good and bad, on future generations. It also clearly speaks to the actions of those who've gone before and how their decisions can affect us. This goes all the way back to the ramifications of the sins of Adam and Eve and the obedience of Noah! There's more at stake than just us! If you're a first-generation Christian, there's likely a *lot* of spiritual cleaning that needs to be done in comparison to one who is a third or fourth generation Christian. For the latter, much good has likely preceded them, and they are reaping, even if blissfully unaware, the benefits of having been born into a Christian family.

The way I see it, the more I can do to leave a blessed spiritual inheritance to those who follow, the better. Even if you don't have children, you still have a responsibility to leave this world better than it was before you showed up! Break curses, pray for the land and the lost, for orphaned children and lonely widows. See who and what God puts in your path and how you might make a difference to those people, communities, or nations. God can and will use you!

I recall being asked by God to guide and mentor a young woman who was struggling with a number of issues. At the time, I was coming down off the high of having seen nearly a thousand souls saved, and I was focused on doing the "big" stuff, but I agreed to this assignment. As the months and years passed, I could see growth in this young woman, and it was gratifying to know that God had given me an opportunity to make a difference in her life.

> He taught me what it is to disciple, what it is to help a person grow from infancy to maturity in the faith.

Participating in the process gave me joy and satisfaction, demonstrating to me that whatever the role, it's important. Whether one life was changed or a few hundred souls were saved, it's about living in obedience to the King.

As I sought to do His will, I longed to be used by God in any way possible. I became like a sponge, soaking and gleaning all that I could from whoever was willing to share. At first glance this might appear to be a good thing, but it wasn't, primarily because of my somewhat random and indiscriminate choices of those from whom I chose to receive this education. Although well-intentioned, the advice given from one often conflicted with the advice from another, and in some cases the counsel given was completely contrary to scripture. I found myself in a bit of a "quandary," for want of a better word. Clarity came as I became stronger in knowledge and understanding by way of the Word.

As I became more deeply rooted in faith, I was no longer tossed to and fro by various opinions, teachings, and doctrines. It's so important to become grounded in the Word as soon as possible so that we can hold fast to truth. Scripture tells us to add to that faith virtue, knowledge, self-control, perseverance, godliness, brotherly kindness, and love. We're even promised that if we diligently abide by these guidelines, we will never stumble. That's definitely the best advice ever! When secure in our faith, it becomes far easier to hear from and trust in God.

Reflections

Have you had any personal experience with acting in/exercising faith?

Can you think of a time when God asked something of you? How did you respond?

FOUR

Growing in Faith

HIS WAY

And so, having grown in faith, trusted in the Lord, and acted in obedience through the releasing of the business (actually a ministry), it was an *ending* to a three-and-a-half-year run of evangelistic concerts and the beginning of something new.

I wasn't quite sure what the something new would be. However, once the decision had been made to *not* continue down the same road with the concerts, but to stop and seek God and *His* plan, came the waiting, the associated frustration, and even despair. I created and founded a charitable trust through which ministry opportunities could be birthed, but otherwise I found this to be a very quiet season. Nine long months would pass with no real visible movement. There was spiritual growth. There was continued confirmation that God would use music to reach souls. There was opportunity for me to sing again, and this was an incredible gift, considering I'd been unable to sing for years due to stage anxiety issues that sharply halted my opera career in the late eighties.

Then it happened. I received a phone call. It was Tom Howard (R.I.P.), a music arranger and director from Nashville, saying he'd like to come back to Canada to record an album and wanted to work with our fabulous two-hundred-voice choir, soloists, and house band! At long last there was light at the end of the tunnel.

We agreed to do something mutually beneficial, although I'm fairly certain that thanks to his gracious offer, my benefit was far greater. We were able to plan for their recording and then our concert. The latter would take the form of a worship gala, which would give us the means to present to the believing community the reasoning behind what had been accomplished in the past and also the opportunity to share our dreams for the future. I not only wanted to relate the vision God had placed on my heart to the people of our city but also bring praise and worship to the One at the centre of that vision.

In short, the whole worship gala from beginning to end was of God. Everything from the date it was held (the middle of a world games sporting event) to the location (central to the games and the city) to those involved (multiple churches represented, thereby seeing unity) to absolutely everything! I had waited, not always patiently, and then God had spoken, and it was all completely wonderful, just as promised in Psalm 27:14: *"Wait on the Lord; be of good courage, and He shall strengthen your heart; Wait, I say, on the Lord!"*

> But my faith was tested by a phone call
> that brought me to my knees.

There were only a few days to go until show time. Customarily, I was known to keep a watchful eye on ticket sales, but because the event had been fully sponsored and we had so many participants involved in the production, I hadn't stewed over sales.

You see, participants generally aid in filling the venue by inviting their friends. The hall I'd booked for the concert was a magnificent, brand-new, 1,600-seat, state-of-the-art theatre managed by a good friend of mine. I was completely stunned when my colleague from the concert hall called to advise me that only sixty tickets had been sold and then asked if I would like to cancel the event! I was so taken aback that I could barely speak.

I managed to eke out some sort of a response, but the shock of what he'd just said stopped me dead in my tracks. I couldn't fathom that this was happening. Disappointment ... discouragement ... and embarrassment enveloped me. My mind raced as I considered the worst-case scenario. If I chose to proceed, it would mean having more than three times as many people on the stage than in the audience! I was horrified. My stomach was in my throat.

So here I was, faced yet again with another step of faith. If this truly was of God, and only sixty people were to be there, then who was I to shut it down? I had to push pride and humiliation aside, and although career suicide was staring me straight in the face, it was evident that this was not my decision to make.

Keep in mind I'd had to "believe" for miracles before (in terms of warm bodies in seats), and although other miracles had been realized, they weren't always the ones associated with the warm bodies. I was quite literally believing for the best and yet preparing for the worst, knowing that at the end of the day, it would be God's vision realized and not necessarily mine.

I was keenly aware that God resists the proud but gives grace to the humble, and I needed to humble myself. My faith needed to be in God and in His work being accomplished—not in the number of people who may or may not show up! Although this might not sound like a very big deal, it was a challenging obstacle to overcome.

Many colleagues from the world were watching this with a critical eye as were, unfortunately, even more critics from within Christian circles, most of whom had already given up on me! Well, I have to say, not only was God's presence felt by those on stage but also by the eleven-hundred-plus people who attended that evening. They were lined up all around the concert hall outside the building, clamouring for tickets. As a matter of fact, we had to start the gala late in order to get everyone into the venue!

As I reflect back on it, this evening was also the beginning of Him separating the wheat from the chaff: those who saw God in all of this, and those who looked upon it with worldly or fleshly eyes and could not see, as if blinded by some sort of jealousy or pride. God was clearly present, yet the nay-sayers, with cynicism and judgment in their hearts, had made up their minds about me and this ministry. What followed was truly ugly and vicious, as gossip and rumours abounded. It was painful beyond belief, and I almost didn't make it out. But, as only God can do,

> He in all grace and mercy made me stronger, with even greater conviction that although grievous at times, this walk of faith greatly pleased Him.

Many of my friends had rejected me. My husband was working out of town. It was me, my small children, and very few faithful friends. I was alone. I mourned, and something inside me died. I threw myself into praying and reading the Word. I was consumed by God and His goodness and a growing, insatiable desire to go deeper. In spite of all the criticism, or perhaps as a result of it, I was emerging stronger than ever. My perseverance in the faith was being rewarded, and I began to recognize that as faith grows, we might be entrusted with a vision. When this happens, we'll know Him well enough to know that it's *Him* speaking.

Hearing, seeing, or sensing an undeniable message is where the real fun begins! When He places these jewels into our hearts, we can rest assured that in due season, His promises will be accomplished. Although not all the patriarchs were able to see these visions, dreams, and promises through to completion in their lifetimes, how beautiful it is when blessed by God with the opportunity to witness His vision unfold before us!

> I am one of the blessed, having observed the fulfillment of many a promise.

On this particular occasion, however, prior to that glorious time, I was required to live and move amongst those who had turned their backs on our family. This meant facing rejection over and over again, each and every week at church, without being released to move on. Throughout this time of suffering, I was given a greater understanding and appreciation of the pain Jesus endured at the betrayal of Judas, and even more so by the denial of His dear friend, Peter. It was incredibly agonizing. I drew my strength from my faith and experienced some mighty miracles.

I continued to sing and was blessed to lead a music ministry that frequently visited a maximum-security prison for young offenders. We served there for about three years, ultimately seeing quite a large number of youth come to Christ. It was freeing to be there and to minister to these kids. Strangely, there was far more love at the prison than at the church I attended.

Although I was completely aware that many of the crimes executed were cruel and heinous acts, I chose to remain focused on the broken hearts and souls before me. A large percentage of these kids had fetal alcohol syndrome (something imposed upon them in the womb by their drinking mothers), and even more of them had been sexually abused (also something inflicted upon them). Their young lives had been wracked with pain that had turned to anger, resulting in sin and, eventually, severe punishment.

But here's the crazy part. Not only did most of them never get a fair shot at life, but sadly, once in prison, many preferred this life, feeling safer and more protected in jail than they were at home. This broke my heart. Over the years of ministering there, I often felt that they helped me more than I helped them. They were so appreciative of what we were doing, craving the warmth and acceptance we were able to provide thanks to God's incredible grace and mercy operating in our own lives.

Over this same course of time, there remained a small group of us who continued to pray for opportunities to bring God's love through music to the masses, in His time and in His way, *just* as had been revealed to us at the very beginning through that prophetic word. And then it happened. We got the green light *and* we received *all* the funding necessary to produce a professional gospel music festival, free admission and all, bringing God's music right into the centre of a community, in a public park, within a stone's throw of a huge public market where people of every shape, size, colour, age, and background had the option to listen or not. We prayed for an event that would be simple in its goals and structure yet excellent in its execution.

We wanted to share the love of Christ through the music.

With the purpose being so evangelistic and outreach-oriented, it was a complete answer to prayer that this event could be produced with no charge, no hidden agenda, no angle, no pressure. Hmm, kinda like God's gift of redemption! Well, God put everything into motion, including the desire to pray for this in the first place!

As I said, there was miraculous funding and there were volunteers hand-picked by the King Himself. There were musicians and artists, all of whom were Canadian, all professional and loving the Lord, with a desire to reach the lost. God chose the location and the date. He touched hearts to give, participate, and donate until every need was met. What a blessing to be chosen to serve on such a God-ordained event. There was prayer, and prayer, and then some more prayer as the big day approached.

The day before the festival, there was much to be done. A stage, with a roof and all, needed to be built from scratch. This meant hours of labour in the hot sun, and I mean hot sun! Heavy duty equipment had to be brought in, barrels of water from the city, with trucks of all sorts coming and going throughout the day bringing portable toilets, tents, sound gear, lighting gear, catering gear, merchandise, security, and more. People were working and cleaning, and, yes, even laughing for hours and hours until everything was ready to go the next morning. The team leaders and their crews were all absolutely amazing. Their exuberant attitudes were such a blessing, because even when something didn't work out as smoothly as hoped, there was always a sense of determination, camaraderie, and faith.

> It was a labour of love, and a dream and a prophesy come
> to fruition. God is so faithful.

It was a day of miracles, a day I have never forgotten. Thousands were in attendance, and God blessed our socks off with loads of precious memories and countless treasured stories.

One woman in particular caught a volunteer's attention as she sat weeping in the shade of the trees. She had awakened that morning, jumped into her car, and started driving, with no idea as to why she had done this, nor any clue as to her destination. Miraculously, this is where she ended up! Her child had recently passed away, and as she sat there mourning this unimaginable loss, she was aware of Jesus' comforting presence.

We were also deeply moved by a sixteen-year-old who had been so badly beaten by his stepfather that he had suffered long-term effects mentally, physically, and spiritually. That day he experienced the beginnings of spiritual freedom as team members spent time talking and praying with him. It was inspiring to see his countenance change as the day progressed.

I was also touched by the story of a woman and her child who had been on a nearby bike path. She stopped to listen and found herself engaged in a conversation in which she openly confessed her involvement in a cult and how desperately she desired freedom. The long day ended with another young man asking how he could turn his life over to Christ. Thousands came and went throughout the day, and we witnessed perhaps one of the longest conga lines ever. Hundreds jumped to their feet to dance and sing and praise in a public park! Our prayer-and-book tent was constantly active: children were getting their faces painted, food was plentiful, and laughter widespread. We were greatly encouraged by the opportunities bestowed upon us to share the love of Christ with those whom God had sent.

Praise be to God!
"He who calls you is faithful, who also will do it."
(1 Thessalonians 5:24)

ROLLER COASTER

At long last we were released to join a new church family, and it was here, amongst these believers, that I would experience healing from the rejection previously suffered. I'd also sit under some wonderful teaching. Incredibly, during this period of time, I also ended up experiencing both extremes of that roller coaster ride. I'll begin with the "lows," the completely bizarre things that started happening to me physically. Out of the blue, I began to have some highly peculiar swelling occurrences. These "episodes," I'll call them, didn't take long in progressing so that within a relatively short period of time, my entire face grew into a full-blown distorted mess. The swelling was usually so severe that I was virtually unrecognizable, even to friends.

One day, a complete stranger who had seen me in my parked vehicle approached, offering to take me to the women's shelter because she thought I'd been beaten! Sometimes one or both of my eyes would be fully swollen shut. My lips looked as though I'd had a very scary encounter with a collagen-filled needle in the hands of a mad doctor, and my cheeks were so swollen that the blood vessels on my face had begun to break!

> I gained just a small understanding of what it must do to
> a person's sense of self when struck
> with a disease like leprosy.

When looking like this, one becomes completely torn as to how to even attempt to live a normal existence. If I went out in public, I was devoid of any confidence and absolutely lacking in self-esteem. On the other hand, if I stayed inside, ensuring that I steered clear of mirrors or reflective devices of any kind, then I risked falling into an incredible depression in my "woe is me, pity party for one" place of solitude.

The other obvious part of this scenario is that I was still a wife and mother, and I had responsibilities, so I tried to achieve balance. When things needed to get done outside my home, I simply donned a baseball cap and sunglasses and did the best I could to frighten the least number of people possible.

Throughout this season came many visits to the doctor, the hospital, the laboratory, the pharmacist, specialists, and essentially all the people who test, poke, prod, and medicate you to try to find out what's happening. The obvious conclusion that this was an allergic reaction didn't appear to be the answer. I do have many allergies, but the medical professionals didn't believe this was the reason for my extreme swelling.

Then along came a new reality. The former external swelling, which could last for a week or more, didn't seem to be happening as frequently on my face but had now moved inwards and was attacking me internally.

> The good news was that I didn't look nearly so
> frightening, but the bad news was that it could
> now be life-threatening!

In the beginning, I didn't know this critical (i.e. life-threatening) piece of information, so my first new encounter with this "development" was, if

I do say so myself, quite comical and has, even long after the fact, caused me to chuckle at its remembrance.

The first time that I noticed something new and different happening to me was in the middle of the night. I awoke to discover that my tongue was swollen—really swollen! How odd, I thought. How did I manage this? Did I bite it in my sleep?

I stumbled out of bed to get a closer look, and what I saw in my bathroom mirror corroborated my assumptions that my tongue had, in fact, more than doubled in size! I decided to call a twenty-four-hour medical hotline to get their opinion. A nurse took my call, and although my speech didn't possess its usual clarity, she really didn't seem troubled.

I was about to climb back into bed when it became painfully obvious that my tongue was continuing to swell. It was clear I needed to get to the hospital. I was frustrated by what a nuisance this had become. I'd spent quite a lot of time at this hospital and was growing weary of the whole situation. It wouldn't be long before my family awakened, and I was keenly aware they would need to use the van—our one and only vehicle. It seemed that the least disruptive way to handle things would be for me to ride my daughter's bike over to the hospital, which was only three to four kilometres away (about two to two-and-a-half miles for the non-metric crowd). This way the rest of the family could carry on as usual. Easy! So I got dressed, donned a helmet, and off I went.

While riding, I realized that I was deteriorating quite rapidly and had become increasingly unstable. Although my vitals were declining, I remained calm and made it to the hospital.

Now, to get the full effect here, you have to picture the nurse at the emergency reception desk watching someone cycle into the building, park her "wheels," calmly remove her helmet, and casually wander up to the desk. Naturally, she just carried on with what she was doing, not terribly concerned about the cyclist in front of her. With her head still down, she began to fill out a form for me, asking for my name.

By this point, I was actually in very bad shape and couldn't even speak because my tongue was so swollen and my system was completely out of whack. Nonetheless, I made what I would consider to be a respectable attempt to say my name, which of course was completely unrecognizable and sounded as though I had a speech impediment. Confused, and seemingly annoyed, the nurse slowly raised her head as I was opening my mouth to point to the enormity of my tongue. Well, the rest is a bit of a blur.

I was pretty much thrown onto a stretcher and injected with more epinephrine than ever before or after, steroids and whatnot, nearly launching me through the roof! Between the medication, the heart and blood pressure monitoring, the oxygen and more, what I had thought to be a rather humorous, albeit annoying, predicament was not met with the same sense of amusement by the medical community. I was sympathetic to their perspective, given that they nearly had to do a tracheotomy, which would <u>not</u> have been good for a singer, but if you could have seen the look on the nurse's face when I arrived, it would have made you laugh, too!

Regardless, I was now moving into new territory, and every episode was different than the previous one, making it very difficult to predict. Sometimes it was my throat, sometimes my esophagus, and other times there would be swelling in some arbitrary location like my leg, arm, or foot. As it turned out, I was diagnosed with something called Acute Idiopathic Angioedema, basically a "random" skin/auto-immune type of disease that no one understands. I was determined to do whatever I could to get well, be healed, and move past this whole thing. However, as time went on, rather than being healed, the list of diseases with which I was diagnosed grew to a place of being utterly ridiculous!

To be honest, it literally felt like the enemy was trying to "take me out," and although I had my "down" days, I was determined to not allow him to mess with me! I felt a definite and growing kinship to Job.

> Throughout the course of my journey to physical healing,
> which was many years in the making,
> came spiritual healing.

I learned about the root causes of disease whilst becoming educated by my brother, also a follower of Christ, on the things I could do in the natural. He had spent years of study and practice in methods that had ultimately brought an end to his struggle with colitis. I went through freedom ministry, continued to speak out words of healing from scripture, turned to natural remedies, and did my utmost to maintain a positive attitude. I wasn't going to allow anything to stop me from serving God or from being a blessing to others whenever possible.

Eventually, I came to the conclusion that although I wasn't fully cured, my healing was in "process." Some healing is immediate, but as a friend used to say, more often than not, it's "pick and shovel healing." It takes time. Of course, I always believed that one day it would "go," and I was resolute in my decision to never give up!

Okay, so now onto the "high" in my roller coaster ride. As the physical and spiritual healing was underway, God blessed me with an incredible opportunity. The communications position that I had left years prior in order to pursue the gospel concerts was with a museum within the provincial government. The museum contacted me because they were going to be having a very significant centennial celebration, complete with performances, displays, media attention, VIPs, and the unveiling of a new name for the museum by Her Majesty, Queen Elizabeth II, during her Royal Visit. Would I like to create and direct the event? Would I?! This was just the boost I needed. After so much pain and discouragement, it was magnificent and affirming to be entrusted with such a significant role!

> I was reminded of how much God wanted to bless me
> and that I was still a worthwhile vessel for His work and
> His will to be accomplished.

So much happened as a result of this post that it's too much to share here, but suffice it to say, it was a real highlight. I knew that God had strategically placed me in this position, and I was privileged to stand before royalty. What an honour to be able to pray for political leaders, policing units, government and cultural organizations, with a real sense of authority attached to those prayers. It was phenomenal to see how God ensured His music and message was a part of this public event; it was a real blessing and demonstration of His favour!

If it's true that what goes up must come down, then even the highs in our lives would be unpleasant, because we'd be unceasingly aware of the fact that a "low" was on its way. What seems to occur more often than not is that we experience both extremes of this crazy ride at the same time! In the midst of this majestic season of my life, working with and moving amidst dignitaries and royalty, our family had hit rock bottom financially. All the concerts and events from the past, some of which had easily cost up to a hundred thousand dollars each, had caught up with us. Because the sponsorships and support hadn't materialized to the extent required, and the ticket sales weren't as plenteous as hoped, we were left holding the bag.

> We had hit the end of the road, and the outlook from where we stood was one of total devastation.

We stood firmly on the Word of the Lord to act in obedience and remain vigilant and aware of the vision I'd received to focus on the souls and not the money. We'd seen miraculous results from the thousands of lives that had been touched. It seemed that we had done everything we could do, and now, after eight long years of toiling and battling on the financial front, we were left with two options. One was a miracle, and the other was bankruptcy. We held on tightly, praying for that miracle until we could literally hang on no longer. We wept and prayed, repented for any errors we may have made along the way, forgave those who had hurt us and blessed those who hadn't given or served when called, and then, with deep sorrow, declared ourselves to be insolvent.

> When people don't obey the nudging of the Holy Spirit
> to get involved in something that God is doing,
> it hurts the whole body.

We couldn't do this alone, yet we were committed to not allow the disobedience of others stop us from doing our part. This was a hefty price to pay. Once all was said and done, we were able to recognize God's goodness, even in this. It was our year of Jubilee. We were being set free, so we thanked the Lord! I also received revelation after the fact that this outcome had been prophesied through the vision I'd had six years earlier. Do you remember the vision of all the money being taken as people were being saved from the fire? It was all part of the plan. This insight brought incredible peace.

Throughout this journey, we repeatedly found ourselves experiencing both hardship and opportunity simultaneously. After my work for The Queen, I was hired to manage an event for our province's Lieutenant Governor (The Queen's representative), and then the opening of a multi-million-dollar sports facility.

It was the best of times. It was the worst of times. Even in the midst of all these trials, in the midst of lack, illness, and discouragement, God was blessing us and using me to impact leaders, those whom He'd placed in my sphere of influence. It's astounding how God uses the unlikely things and people of this world to confound the wise.

TAKING GROUND

I strongly encourage you to pray for those in leadership, whether you support them or not, because our leaders need to be good leaders, regardless of which party, church, or group they represent. To do their jobs well and to be effective for the Kingdom, they need to hear from God.

When we pray for political leaders, teachers, business leaders, youth leaders, and leaders of every kind, we are interceding for them. We're praying that God's will be done, that they will hear His voice and choose to love our Lord and the people they serve more than they do their own personal need to attain position, power, and control. We need to pray that they will be supported, advised, encouraged, and financed by godly people. We need to trust that God can and will use them to carry out His purposes. By praying for them and blessing them rather than cursing them, we make a difference! What's incredible is that we can do this right from the comfort of our own homes!

Maybe some of you are meant to be leaders yourselves or to walk alongside someone else who has been called. Don't discourage those who are willing to make a difference. Even if you don't agree with everything they stand for, be reminded that it's better to have a Christian holding a persuasive position within our world system than to not. Trust me when I say that our leaders receive more than enough input from the world. I've seen this firsthand, and believe me, it's not pretty to watch as a mafia leader finances and influences a politician who was unable to retain his position without the financial support this one was quick to offer. Aren't there any wealthy, godly people who could have supported someone, or have they all run away from the political arena?

Maybe you're not wealthy or political but instead one who could ensure better programming on television or produce clean, family movies. Perhaps you're called to develop a cure or invent some sort of energy-saving device. It's like eating healthy: there needs to be shops that provide good, wholesome food for this to become a viable alternative for folks. When this occurs, it's far more effective to move our business to the healthy food store than it is to picket or write letters complaining about the burger joint down the road. This is what I had tried to do through the music evangelism events.

> My desire was to produce high quality events in a neutral and professional venue, providing an alternative to some less "healthy" choices.

My desire was to produce high quality events in a neutral and professional venue, providing an alternative to some less "healthy" choices.

I enjoyed spending my time doing this and believed that I was encouraging the world to view Christians as people who contributed and didn't just try to "ruin" everyone else's fun. This can be much more effective than being seen as the "naysayers" or complainers. Picketing and petitions can have a positive effect but aren't always the answer.

What I learned was that over time, as I became trusted by my worldly counterparts, I would be given more and more latitude, thereby giving me opportunity to effect positive change within these secular environments. I beseech you to not only lobby and petition but to initiate, provide, or support godly alternatives.

If the appropriate action isn't obvious, then get a group of intercessors together to pray for revelation about how God wants you to proceed. Maybe the issue or problem needs to be resolved differently than how you originally thought. Let God have His say in the matter.

Unfortunately, as a result of political correctness, we live and work in environments where absolutely everyone and everything is tolerated *except* Christianity. I have encountered an incredible lack of respect from people of other faiths who have made rude comments about my beliefs, causing me to wonder not only at the inappropriateness of this behaviour but at the fact that such conduct would never be accepted should the roles be reversed.

There's a double standard at work, but regardless of how we're treated, we Christians are required to love. We are called to love everyone, even though we may not agree. Loving, however, does not mean that we are to concede.

We are *never* to deny our faith.

As a matter of fact, if we deny Christ before man, He will deny us before our Heavenly Father. That's a stiff penalty. This is why church leaders need to exercise extreme discernment about what things to remain firm in (God's ways, God's Word, Jesus' sacrifice, Holy Spirit leading) and what things they need to be flexible on (style, mandate, programs, works, timing). Unfortunately, many institutions have become too steeped in tradition or programs and not immersed enough in God. Others are "in touch" but have watered down the message in order to "reach out," thereby compromising their foundational principles.

A journalist friend of mine, who at the time was a new believer, visited what might be considered a "neutral" church. He was genuinely appalled and vowed never to return, noting that if he was seeking political correctness, he could have just as easily stayed at his office.

> When people are seeking an encounter with truth ...
> with the Lord ... with the Holy Spirit, then they should
> be able to do so in a church that calls itself Christian.

We need to do things God's way, serving and listening to God rather than people. This is precisely what I spoke of earlier. If church leaders are listening to people of influence, and that influence is primarily due to their financial contributions or societal position, then *everything* must be re-evaluated! If "funders" leave, is God big enough to take care of the needs of the church? Is He able to bring in new people who could bless the church? Could He be asking for new leadership? Should your church even exist as it has in the past, or should it become a soup kitchen, youth centre, or a housing complex for the elderly or disadvantaged? Maybe you should be operating a mission centre or a school.

With the new wave of social media, websites, blogs, internet, and so on, the playing field has changed. Pay close attention to these trends. Yes, some may be "fads," but others are the beginning of a new way of life. If you fight against the wrong ones, you could become ineffective and out of touch.

Whatever it is that God is saying, it's far better to be obedient to Him and to His Word than it is to please people and receive His wrath. Let's be willing to stop and listen to the Lord and create something positive, good, and godly. It won't be easy, but by doing so, we can be more effective for His Kingdom work.

Reflections

Have you ever been ostracized because of your faith or your convictions?

How do you cope when unjustly judged?

Have you made judgments about yourself (or others) that you need to rescind or withdraw?

FIVE
Trouble with Faith

STANDING FIRM

Truthfully, there will be discomfort as we walk by faith, but we need to push through and past the hardships that try to discourage us. If you've entered a season that feels like hell, whatever you do, don't wallow in misery there but keep moving. Keep pushing. Keep positive.

When you step up and into the things of God, the heat will inevitably get turned up. Don't let this surprise you. Although obstacles and temptations can get in the way, we must remain strong in the Lord, knowing that God is simply challenging us to grow. Over time, as we mature in the faith, we will be stronger in our resolve to stand for Him, ultimately bringing us to a place of deep and undeniable peace. Although it may seem strange to think that when living for and in obedience to the Prince of Peace we will experience peace within but not necessarily in our environment, it's true!

Bear with me while I try to explain something fairly complex in relation to peace. When we live in obedience to Him, there will be things asked of us that others won't understand. As a result, division can occur. Now, given that unity is a godly principle, this is a bit of a paradox. But here's how it works. When God asks us to speak for Him, stand for Him, or simply choose Him and not dangle in a neutral zone, the harmonious equilibrium previously enjoyed will be shaken. While it's exceedingly difficult to understand how, while attempting to live peaceably and in unity, we may end up separated from those who at one time were once close to us, this is reality. Sometimes it's only for a season, but in other cases, it can be for longer. It could be that we're called to walk different paths, so God needs to separate us in order that we might live out our destinies. Sometimes it could be that these relationships are unhealthy, and their removal is God's protection.

Take a moment to think back to when you first became a believer. In choosing to live for Christ, you likely didn't purposefully turn your back on old friends but probably found that, over time, only a few, if any, remained. Some people pulled away as you changed, and sometimes you pulled away because the environment was poison to your soul. The same thing can result as we grow deeper in faith.

As we stand for Him, things will change.

> *Do not think that I came to bring peace on earth. I did not come to bring peace but a sword. For I have come to set a man against his father, a daughter against her mother, and a daughter-in-law against her mother-in-law.* (Matthew 10:34–35)

So how it is that the "Prince of Peace" didn't come to bring peace?

Well, He *did* come to bring peace: "*Peace I leave with you, my peace I give to you; not as the world gives do I give to you. Let not your heart be troubled, neither let it be afraid*" (John 14:27). However, in this context, He is speaking of a peace that is within us when we live for Him.

The peace He has left us is Holy Spirit peace.
That's different than the division or lack of peace that can occur as we stand for Him and for what is right.

I couldn't believe what I was hearing. Surely I had misunderstood. Had my grandmother actually threatened me? Was she lying to me? Where had all this bigotry and hatred come from? Why was my alcoholic uncle (her son) still living with her—a woman in her eighties? I was struggling to assimilate this peculiar new reality in which I found myself. All I knew was that I needed to call my parents so that I could get clarity, the truth.

I was twenty-four-years-old and had received an invitation to audition for the opera department at the University of Toronto. I thought I'd round out my time in the east by catching up with my grandma. As I lay in bed at her apartment thinking about her outlandish words and actions, it struck me that I had never previously spent time alone with her. Clearly there was a reason for this. What became painfully obvious was that unbeknownst to me, my dad had been raised in a fairly hideous environment. I later discovered that for him to remain steadfast in the faith and also protect himself, his wife, and children, he needed to remove us from that which was unhealthy and, in fact, vile.

I am grateful for what he did. Although he'd experienced some incredibly painful times as a result of these decisions, he stood for what was right, and we all reaped the reward of his resolve by living a peaceful, happy life. Somehow he managed to honour his parents from a great distance while protecting us and the welfare of our family from the ugliness he'd endured while growing up. Because of his stand, my brother and I, our children, and our children's children have an even richer, purer, more Christ-like heritage! So while we all experienced inward peace, the outward ramifications of this stand created division and a lack of peace.

> Every time I am given opportunity to take a stand for God, it's actually a gift in disguise, because it allows me to grow stronger in my faith.

What this means is that each subsequent time something is required of me, even if more difficult than anything I've previously done, it's not such a great leap because my faith has grown, making it well worth the struggle. In all that we do for our Saviour, ultimately we are the ones to receive the reward. It's actually a pretty good deal! Remember, though, that if we choose *not* to stand for Him, we have, even if inadvertently, taken a stand against Him. Just as there are rewards in standing for Him, there are consequences if we don't. Each time we stand for what is right and godly, there is an excellent chance that we will lose some friends and maybe even some family members.

I'd like to share a poem with you, written by Mother Teresa, that's engraved on the wall of her home for children in Calcutta. I love how the author, Kent M. Keith, offers encouragement to keep on fighting the good fight!

> People are often unreasonable, illogical and self-centred; Forgive them anyway.
>
> If you are kind, people may accuse you of selfish ulterior motives; Be kind anyway.
>
> If you are successful, you will win some false friends and some true enemies; Succeed anyway.
>
> If you are honest and frank, people may cheat you; Be honest and frank anyway.
>
> What you spend years building, someone could destroy overnight; Build anyway.
>
> If you find serenity and happiness, they may be jealous; Be happy anyway.
>
> The good you do today, people will often forget tomorrow; Do good anyway.
>
> Give the world the best you have, and it may never be enough; Give the world the best you've got anyway.
>
> You see, in the final analysis, it is between you and God; It was never between you and them anyway.

TRUST

"Trust in the Lord with all your heart, and lean not on your own understanding, in all

> *your ways acknowledge Him, and He shall direct your paths."* (Proverbs 3:5–6)

It's easy to see why folks find it difficult to trust. If we've been disappointed, rejected, or deceived in the past, it can be challenging to let down our guard and trust because we view it as vulnerability. Remember, though, that these negative experiences of the past were with people, not God. Although some may believe that God wasn't there for them when they called on Him, I am here to declare to you that He *was* with you during those difficult days, and He *is* with you now!

It's vitally important that we grasp how incredibly deeply He loves and cares for us. When we weep, He weeps, and when we hurt, He hurts. Alarming horrors take place every day, and frequently the blame for all of this is misplaced. We become angry with God rather than with Satan. We attribute these injustices to God, when absolutely nothing could be further from His character. He has hopes for us, plans for us, wanting us to grow and prosper in all things. Even when He allows tragedy, it has a purpose. The tragedies remind us that we need Him. He wants to ensure that none perish without hope, which is why He sent and subsequently sacrificed His only Son.

This was done so that you and I might be saved from all that is evil. While here on earth, we're unable to escape some of this evil, but we can choose to put our hope and trust in God. We can opt to follow Jesus, knowing that in doing so, our eternal destiny is sealed with Him, allowing us to be forever in His presence. How I'd relish being in a place where there is no more pain or suffering, no more tears, and no more anguish. His love for us is long-suffering and everlasting. Even though we falsely accuse Him, He remains steadfast in His love for us. We just need to say "yes" to that love. Then, as Christ takes up residence in our hearts and our faith is strengthened, we will begin to comprehend the "width and length and depth and height" of His love for us. (See Appendix II).

It's crucial that we sow these truths deep into our hearts. In learning to trust, we mustn't be impatient but be content to move into this reality, one small step at a time. Then, as we learn about our Heavenly Father, His character, and His ways, our growth will accelerate by leaps and bounds. Eventually, these truths will move from our heads to our hearts, and over time, we'll grow in Holy Spirit power. We can't lean on our own understanding, which is limited and fickle. Our "feelings" are unreliable.

> God remains the same, yesterday, today, and forever.
> Now that's something and someone worth trusting!

Don't be hard on yourself. I've known the Lord for decades, and while there are instances and circumstances through which I've had absolutely no difficulty trusting Him, there have been other areas that have completely challenged me. It took me years to release these concerns and burdens, eventually allowing Him to carry the load. This freed me from all sorts of pain and anguish.

It's sad when you think about it, because at the very point and time that we receive His saving power, we also receive freedom, deliverance, and forgiveness, bought and paid for as part of the deal. Somehow I had managed to leave the "shop" without taking what had already been purchased, and that which rightfully belonged to me. From what I've seen, this is very common. We feel greedy taking all that God offers, realizing that the transaction isn't at all equal or fair. We can see that we're not worthy. But that's the point; it's not possible for us to be worthy. It's about God's love and grace and mercy and Jesus' sacrifice for us! It is done. It is finished. There's absolutely nothing we can add to make it more ours.

In not being able to "add," we sometimes leave part of it behind. We decide to forfeit peace by keeping our guilt or hanging on to "works," just in case grace isn't enough. Maybe we choose to hold on to pain and nurse our hurts for a while longer. We don't gratefully and gracefully receive the forgiveness, the healing, and the freedom meant for us. Let's stop this silliness and grab hold of what we've been given. When in Christ, we are in victory! This is why I'm able to put one foot in front of the other. Regardless of my circumstances, I know that God is with me every step of the way. I am never alone, and neither are you. We are all on a journey, each travelling at our own pace down the road to a more Christ-like existence.

From this vantage point, it's critical that we help and not hinder one another, edify and not tear down, give without reserve, and love others as Christ has loved us, freely and selflessly with integrity and honour.

Having personally worked through and overcome many of the obstacles before me, I was at long last emotionally and spiritually healed and ready to be used by God. It was clear in my mind and heart that He was going to move our family to a new location. We just didn't know when or where! For three years we had been alert, watching and waiting for revelation. When it did at long last happen, it happened very quickly, moving us even deeper into this adventurous walk of faith.

I think what might be significant here is that although we knew a move was inevitable, no other information had been revealed to us. What did occur on a fairly consistent basis over this period of time was something I'd liken to a rhythm. It was as though we were being propelled through this phase of the journey in a rather remarkable fashion, constantly sensing that we were being led, guided, and instructed in a new and different way. Over and over again we received just one piece of information or directive at a time. There were no confirmations, only undeniable requests along with a clear expectation that obedience would follow.

> Our faith needed to be proven through obedience before
> we would receive confirmation, which was usually only
> then followed by more direction.

It was a wildly fascinating time that held a striking resemblance to a "suspense" novel, but this was no nail biting, edge-of-your seat book or film but rather our lives! While this season progressed quickly, the time leading up to this spine-tingling chapter had been founded on years of passionate prayer. We had feverishly sought the Lord, died to self, and purposefully and decidedly sown into His Kingdom work.

The initial indication of impending change transpired when the folks with whom we had a housing agreement told us they had been instructed by God to sell our house. We were disappointed but not surprised, given that we knew a move was in our future. Selling this home was, however, far more noteworthy than it may sound. It had been a dream-come-true for us, a blessing and an answer to years of prayer. It was a miracle, and it seemed as though the likelihood of our owning another home was highly improbable yet, with God, not impossible. While recognizing that this had been a generous gift and a truly remarkable blessing, it was also abundantly clear that we needed to hold this blessing with an open hand. We had freely received, and now we were to freely give.

The house sold very quickly, so I immediately jumped into packing. Our kids were busy with school and youth activities, and my husband was playing with his jazz trio at a beautiful resort in the Rocky Mountains a few hours away. It was my task to get things organized. Here's the catch, though: I didn't know where we were moving or what we'd be doing, making it extraordinarily challenging to know how or what to pack. We rented a mobile storage container, filling it with what we *thought* was most important first. Whatever didn't fit, we'd give away…. and that turned out to be a lot!

> In the midst of all the activity, I awakened one morning to hear the words: "Get passports!"

While this should have been my first clue that God was calling us away from Canada, I actually thought it was connected to a music tour for my husband, or perhaps a family vacation.

Five packages of passport forms were laid out before me, and I'd only just begun to fill them out when I realized a fee would be required. Exasperated by what appeared to be a waste of time, I looked heavenward and said, "Lord, we don't even have the money to apply for these! I'm pretty certain I heard you correctly, so if you want us to do this, then I really need some money to come from a source that I'm not expecting and that hasn't already been allocated in our family budget so that I can do this."

That was it. I put everything away and continued on with my packing. The very next morning, the ringing of my telephone rescued me from the mountain of boxes before me. It was a friend whom God had awakened in the night with clear instructions to present us with a financial gift.

My heart began to race, knowing full well that the gift was in relation to the passports. This was obviously important to God, so it needed to be important to me. I committed to completing the paperwork, not fully understanding why this needed to be done, only that I needed to trust the Lord and do my part. When I went down to the passport office to submit everything, I somehow ended up in the "express" line, even though I'd clearly stated to the officials that I wasn't in a rush. Apparently, God had a different plan, and according to His plan, these papers needed to be expedited quickly!

Sure enough, we received our passports in record time. Again, as strange as it may sound, with all the distractions associated with the logistics of moving, we weren't too focused on the significance behind the passports. However, once we were out of our house and far removed from all the busyness, it was a different story.

At this point, we were keenly aware of the fact that we didn't have a home to which we could return. We also didn't know where to enroll the kids in school for the fall, and we just plain didn't know much of anything. We enlisted very few trusted friends to pray for us. Between personal revelation and that of our praying friends, we came to a consensus.

> This move was somehow connected to the land of our fathers, our forefathers, our ancestry.

We began to give serious consideration to a number of places within Canada, which actually encompassed much of the country. Strangely, none of it sounded right. Nothing really struck a chord except for British Columbia, mostly because we had spoken many times about moving there. I started looking for work in all the locations that came to mind, hoping to receive insight, but nothing fell into place. As a matter of fact, one day when I went to the computer to begin my search for work, it was as though my fingers were frozen on the keys, and I sensed God say, "Stop, you're looking in the wrong place." What? How could I be looking in the wrong place when I was looking in so many places (in Canada)? So I tried again, but the same thing happened—my fingers were frozen. With this, I stepped away from the computer.

Over the coming days, I was reminded of those words spoken by God to Abraham:

> ... *Get out of your country, from your family and from your father's house, to a land that I will show you ... I will bless you ... and you shall be a blessing. I will bless those who bless you, and I will curse him who curses you ...* (Genesis 12:1–3)

UNDERSTANDING

One day not too long after this, I was having a conversation with one of our praying friends about how baffling this had become. I laughingly said, in a sort of off-the-cuff manner, "Well, if we're really talking ancestry, then the place we're talking about is Scotland!"

Silence ... and more silence.

Oddly enough, this actually made my spirit jump. As the days passed, it really began to sink in that what I originally thought was outlandish might actually be "it!" Most of our ancestors were from the United Kingdom. My husband had family from Antrim, Ireland, and somewhere in Scotland. My mom's parents were from Huntly, Scotland, while my dad's grandparents were from somewhere in Britain.

I won't detail absolutely every confirmation we received, but there were so many, it became ridiculous. I reflected on my childhood, much of it having been filled with all things Scottish, including ten years of performing, competing, and teaching Highland Dancing. I'd even danced for Canada's Prime Minister! I'd played drums in the pipe band, and my brother was a world-class piper. As incredible as all of this was, I needed to remain calm and rational. Our focus had to be on God and what He was saying. Was this the reason we needed those passports? Hmmm ...

We began to look into how one could live and work in Scotland and discovered, of all things, Ancestry Visas! At this point, we decided to call my brother, who had actually been to Scotland, to see if we could gain some insight from him. I was a little apprehensive to tell him what we believed God was asking of us, not knowing how he would react to something so seemingly far-fetched. Instead, he completely took me aback by telling me that a few years earlier, our mom had come across our grandmother's Scottish birth certificate. This "find" instigated a whole string of events that culminated in her having pulled together all the necessary documentation so that my brother could, if required, move to Scotland himself. All of this activity had taken an entire year to accomplish, and I was privy to none of it!

At this point, my brother said, "I don't think it was for me. I think it was for you!" We were reeling! God had a plan for us, and it had been in process for a very long time. Amazing! We called my mom and, sure enough, she had everything.

> Absolutely all that we would require to apply for Ancestry Visas was in my mom's possession.

That was confirmation enough for us. Once again, though, we were hit with another financial roadblock. We didn't have the funds to apply for the visas, so we prayed quite simply, "Lord, if this is of you, we need the money."

I won't go into all the specifics, but by the afternoon of the following day, we had enough funds for the applications, plane tickets, train tickets, container shipping fee, and a few months' rent. As additional confirmation on top of all of this, it materialized in an unsolicited manner—other than our prayers! We were now completely and utterly awestruck. Could this really be happening? We pulled together all the paperwork for the visa applications, prayed, and couriered them off. Now I kid you not—four days later, we had Ancestry Visas in our hands for all five of us! Everything was moving at lightning speed. I started looking for work in Scotland and found two potential positions, one in Edinburgh and one in Inverness, so I applied for both.

It was time to talk to our kids. A lot of prayer had gone on prior to this moment. We believed God was preparing their hearts and that this move was as much about them as about us, although ultimately, we knew that it was all about Him!

With some very real trepidation, we sat down with our three teenagers. At this point, something truly unheard of happened, something that could only be God. Although the conversation almost (I stress the word "almost") went downhill at one point, the news was received far better than we could have ever hoped or imagined! Given that we were removing our teens from all that they had ever known, away from their schools and friends, their tremendous attitudes were an answer to prayer! We told them that from here on out, we'd be "in it" together.

> We knew that God wanted our children to experience
> this journey of faith firsthand, and wouldn't you know it,
> they took to it like ducks to water!

We shared the news with Kevin's family, his bandmates, and somewhere in the midst of all of this, my parents decided to come and see us. Although the time with them was short, we savoured every moment but became concerned at my dad's mention of having found a lump in his arm. As my parents headed back home to get Dad a medical check-up, I received notification that the job for which I'd applied in Edinburgh had been awarded to another candidate. That was the bad news. The good news, however, was that I learned I had been short-listed for the job in Inverness and that I was to be interviewed via telephone. The interview went well, but I would be required to wait another two weeks before finding out whether or not I was successful. Time was running out. I was focused on the time element not only because Kevin's contract, which included our temporary home, would be coming to an end, but also due to the very real dilemma of getting our kids enrolled at a school.

Given that it was now completely obvious we were going to Scotland, we could see that it was time to take another step of faith. Although we hadn't yet received confirmation as to the precise location of our destination, nor did we have jobs or a home, we knew it was time to send our container of belongings. We made plans to go back to our hometown and prepared to itemize, list, and move everything from the first storage unit to the overseas container.

> There was something strangely final associated with this seemingly radical act!

We were at a crossroads, needing to decide on a port, all the while not knowing if I had gotten the job from my recent interview. We prayed, sought God, conferred with the kids, and realized that just as had been our experience throughout this entire process, the next move was ours. So with that, we decided to carry on with plans to move to Inverness, Scotland, the gateway to the Highlands. If we were wrong, then we'd have our container trucked to the appropriate location once we arrived.

This was quite nerve-wracking, because although we felt complete peace in terms of Scotland, we still didn't feel settled on which community. When speaking with the overseas shipping company, the agent seemed surprised when I said that we needed our things to go to Inverness. Apparently, Inverness wasn't one of the more popular ports, but she knew of it because her husband had just returned from working there and had said "it was the most beautiful place" he'd ever been. What an endorsement!

This meant that another phase in the moving saga was upon us. This time we were emptying our temporary little home in the Rockies. Suffice it to say, there was a lot of coordination involved throughout the entire process, yet everything flowed better than I could have ever thought possible. There were moments, of course, when we felt overwhelmed by the sheer volume of activity (physical, emotional, and spiritual), but the underlying sense throughout this entire season was one of complete peace, calm, and protection. Because God mobilized everything so quickly, almost no one knew what was happening, which turned out to be a blessing.

> This time we were able to be "quietly" obedient and live
> by faith without the agenda-ridden questions,
> unkind comments, and spiritual attacks we'd
> previously experienced.

I sensed a protective bubble of some kind around us. I had never known anything quite like it before, but whatever it was, it was of God, and it literally carried us hour by hour and day by day throughout this entire process. When the time came to actually do the container "transfer," it turned out that I was at a women's conference in a completely different city listening to a speaker from … well … Scotland. No, that was *not* planned, but yet further confirmation. This meant that it would just be Kevin and a few other guys to deal with the rather daunting task of moving and itemizing all that was in the storage unit.

What became truly significant about this day was the confirmation that came through one of our friends who had unexpectedly dropped by the storage lot to help with the move. In the midst of all the "grunt" work, our friend asked where the container was going. "Scotland," was Kevin's vague and elusive reply. Our friend asked him to be more specific, so Kevin sheepishly responded with, "Inverness, but we're still not sure."

As soon as this fellow heard the location, he enthusiastically replied, "Yes, it's Inverness, that's where you're going! God spoke to me and told me you'd be moving to Inverness, but I wasn't permitted to say it, only confirm it." That he did.

Once our family was reunited and back in our mountain retreat, the calls from the slightly expanded prayer team began to pour in. They all had the same message: You need to leave soon. Don't delay. Don't hesitate. It's not about the job; you just need to go!

We were sensing the exact same thing. In fact, we were getting so convicted in our spirits that we were almost crawling out of our skins, knowing that the time had come to leave. We were well aware that news would travel fast and reactions would be vast and varied. We also knew there would be a plethora of criticism, just as in the past. Our biggest faith step to date would surely cause some dissention, but what we came to terms with early on was that it really didn't matter. I pictured the day when I would stand before my Father in heaven, giving my account. I imagined Him asking me, "Why didn't you obey me?" followed by my miserable reply of, "Well ... I thought everyone would think I was crazy!" I realized how pathetic this sounded and so resolved, once again, to not concern myself with the reactions of others.

> I re-learned the lesson that fear of man wasn't going to get me anywhere good or godly.

We paused for a moment to take in the beauty of the brilliant sun shimmering off the gorgeous aqua blue lake before us. It really was a stunning sight to behold. We chuckled over comments made by one of the musicians in Kevin's trio, who would walk outside, stretch, look at the gorgeous view, and then, with his completely unique, dry, quick-witted sense of humour, exclaim, "Wow, what a dump!" We laughed. The crystal-clear lake, perfectly nestled into the comforting embrace of the Canadian Rockies, although familiar to us, was still breathtaking. I had walked this path nearly every day for eight gorgeous summers.

This was our second home, and we loved it. We continued along the shaded path, dotted with warmth from the sun, the reality of what we were about to do never far from our minds. I could feel the conviction in my spirit that it was "time," and although Kevin did too, I was impressed by his calm and peaceful demeanour. He was giving up so much. We all were! We considered the beauty of this place and all the years and painstaking effort it had taken to come this far in the music industry, including the connections and the friendships, the kids, their friends and activities. God was asking us to leave it all behind. We quickly shifted our thoughts to the here and now. We couldn't afford to reminisce too long. Our focus needed to be on the task at hand. We were being called away, and that was that.

It was time to go! Kevin gave the final word that he'd be leaving his much-coveted music gig at the resort by the end of the week. We would be leaving the country the week after that! It was all absolutely surreal! Strangely, as only God can orchestrate these things, the day after he'd given notice, I received a letter:

Dear Deborah,

Thank you for taking part in the telephone interview for the above post last week. I am sorry to have to tell you that we have now offered the post to another candidate, who has accepted.

I had been unsuccessful in the job competition in Inverness. And we were moving our family to Inverness the next week! How exceptionally bizarre the timing was. If we had gotten the letter a day earlier, we might have seen it as a sign that we hadn't yet found the correct location. Given that we knew this move "wasn't about the job," Kevin had already given his notice, our belongings were already being shipped to Inverness, and our van had been returned to those who'd originally gifted it. We were headlong into this thing, this move, and this faith walk big time! Through it all though, I'll say it once again, we had a completely undeniable sense of peace.

In the natural, this move would have been completely insane, but that's the beauty of the story. We weren't living according to the flesh. Admittedly, there were times when we'd catch ourselves focused on the things of this world. However, we noted that whenever in this state, the peace of God seemed to slip away. We desperately wanted that peace in our lives, so we immediately self-corrected and got back on the path of living according to the Spirit. I was frequently reminded of when Peter walked on the water. When his eyes were fixed on Jesus, he was bold and confident, but when he looked down at his situation in the natural (water beneath his feet), he began to panic and sink. So in the natural, we were leaving our home, work, family, friends, and country behind.

We were on our way to Scotland, a place we'd never been, with three teenagers and no home, no job, no friends, no family, no church, no ministry team, and no idea what God wanted us to do there.

Okay, that was in the natural. In the spiritual, however, we really weren't any different than those in scripture who had left all simply because it was required of them. "*... And he went out, not knowing where he was going. By faith he dwelt in the land of promise as in a foreign country ...*" (Hebrews 11:8–9).

At one point God had impressed upon my heart, by way of a picture, the choices before me and how I might want to choose to handle the situation. In this image, it looked as though I was standing on a rocky iceberg with a definite, enlarging crack that was breaking apart and into two distinct pieces. I had one foot on each side. As it began to separate, it was becoming increasingly uncomfortable—almost to the place where I would be doing the splits. Because this skill is not in my repertoire of abilities, it would have been excruciatingly painful! God was showing me that I had one foot in the natural while the other was in the spiritual. Eventually I needed to choose by moving one of my feet to join the other. That day I chose the spiritual and realized that life would never again be the same—a good thing, because "*It is the Spirit who gives life; the flesh profits nothing*" (John 6:63a).

> *We were on our way to Scotland, a place we'd never been, with three teenagers and no home, no job, no friends, no family, no church, no ministry team, and no idea what God wanted us to do there.*

Reflections

How do you think a life of faith should look?

Have you experienced or witnessed faith that made you uncomfortable?

Do you find it difficult to trust God?

SIX

Radical Faith

HOW FAR IS TOO FAR?

So what happens when you can't shake the feeling that a friend or acquaintance has taken their faith walk too far? How far is too far? Who determines where this invisible line might be and what it should look like? We know quite a few families who have a large number of children, and I'm reflecting on a conversation I had with a friend who has nine kids. We were discussing how funny it is that people tend to freely offer their opinions, usually without being asked and, in some cases, without even being known. I was telling her how we had received criticism about, of all things, having had our three children so close together.

I was completely mystified as to why others, especially strangers, would even care. This made me wonder about the comments a mother of nine would receive. She said, "You know, I'm not allowed to be tired. When I had one or two babies, it wasn't only okay that I be tired, but it was expected." But as the number of children increased, the compassion toward her decreased. Why is that? Why is it that having two kids is okay but nine is too many, or that a little faith is all right, but if you take it too far, you're on your own?

> I am perplexed as to why when a person is called to carry a heavy burden, others step away rather than stepping up.

Worse than this are the misguided comments and criticisms that ultimately make the load even heavier! At one point in my walk, I was maligned by a friend and church leader who maliciously pronounced, "What you call faith I call stupidity!" Daggers pierced my heart. Daggers thrown by a friend.

Over the ensuing weeks, he went on to boast to others about his witty repartee, turning a bad situation into a truly vicious attack. He had never witnessed faith in action, so his unfortunate response to seeing it live and in person was one of repulsion and disgust. Sometimes the resistance to faith isn't so blatant. There are occasions when despite having seen God move, people are resolute in their stance, digging in their heels, refusing to repent. In the end, though, we see from scripture that it is by faith and faith alone that we will overcome. Living by faith pleases God, and that's good enough for me.

> People desire a comfortable life. They're unable to
> come to terms with how a true walk of faith
> will fit their current lifestyle.
> Well … simply put … it won't!

Sowing and reaping in faith is also a difficult concept for many. In a culture that prides itself on "work," it's troubling for onlookers to come to terms with a walk of faith that God chooses to bless. When God blesses people based on His grace and their obedience and not on "works," it messes with people's minds. Right from the moment we committed to live for God, and without the benefits associated with being a formal pastor or missionary, we were frequently in a position of lack.

Most thought we should raise the white flag, lay down our swords, admit defeat, and call it a day, but we refused. We knew this was the road less travelled and a narrow path leading to the eye of the needle, meaning it would be difficult. We also knew we were wholly and wonderfully directly in the centre of God's will for our lives.

> We had come to terms with the fact that our lives were
> no longer our own but that they belonged to Him.

Therefore, we needed to trust and believe for the miraculous. Again, those watching had a difficult time assimilating what was happening, especially *after* we started to receive those things for which we'd believed.

They felt we needed to "work" for these blessings. What's funny, though, is that we were working! In fact, we were working very hard, but it was for the King of kings and the Lord of lords and not for a company, a business, or a church. This was too difficult a concept for many to comprehend.

One example of this came during the concert days when, as I alluded to earlier, we desperately needed a replacement vehicle. Our poor, tired station wagon was nearing the end of its life, so for three years we prayed consistently, regularly, and specifically for a blue van. We were even planning, in faith, a trip across the country to visit Kevin's family, believing that God would provide us with a safe, large vehicle with which we could take this long-overdue trip. Well, wouldn't you know it, about nine days before we were set to leave, we received news that the Lord had impressed upon someone's heart to buy us a van of our choice!

When we got to the auto lot, chosen by God, we saw two vans side by side, one blue and one green. The green one was not only newer but also in far better condition. We were stumped, trying to negotiate in our little itty-bitty minds how this could be. We had prayed for a blue van. Then, as only God could ordain these things, our salesman, a Christian friend, said, "Well, you can have the blue van that you prayed for or you can have something better that God picked out; it's your choice." We took the green van and never forgot those words. Interestingly, years later, we received a van on a long-term loan from friends, and it was blue!

When we received the green van, there were some who witnessed this rather extraordinary gift as too much to grasp, while for others it was encouraging. Years later, though, when God provided us with that home—the one we were blessed to "rent-to-own" before leaving for Scotland—many who had been okay with us receiving the van were not okay with us receiving the home. Why is that?

> Why do we limit God? Why do we put a ceiling on what He can accomplish?

Why would grace begin and end with salvation? In fact, grace extends well beyond salvation.

> Jesus' death and resurrection brought grace;
> it didn't stop grace.

Because of this inherent misunderstanding, it causes great unrest that our family has received such miracles. I don't think it's because we're any more special than the next person. I think it's simply because we believe in a great big God, for whom *nothing* is impossible! We believe He is who He says He is and that He'll do what He says He'll do. He keeps His word, so we do what's asked of us, knowing He will care for us. It's actually strange to me that people trust the government, their bosses, and the companies they work for more than they trust God. If the company you work for says that they'll take care of you, why wouldn't the God of heaven and earth, who created you, do the same and more?

> God is in the business of miracles.
> We don't just believe for them ... we rely on them.

All the members in our family have experienced physical healing. We have seen financial miracles, been blessed with a number of extravagant gifts, and even lived through a few near-death experiences. Here's the funny thing, though. Even with all this, there have been times when I've believed for the big things but not the little things.

I was in my element and loving every opportunity that came my way to sing with my group of friends. We were scheduled to perform at a radio-thon, and wouldn't you know it, I had laryngitis. I found myself somewhat resigned to this unfortunate fact and assumed we would work around it somehow.

The morning of the gig, I realized that I hadn't actually trusted God to heal my voice. So I prayed and asked for healing so that I might sing at the event. Although nothing seemed to have changed, in faith I prepared and headed over to the event, still with no voice. I went up onto the platform, and wouldn't you know it, He gave me my voice for the songs we were singing, and then it was gone again! I learned a couple vital lessons as a result of this day.

First, I realized I shouldn't only trust God for the big things but also the little things, and, secondly, I should have believed for complete healing and not just for the event!

I choose to believe God can use us to reach entire communities or nations, or even the whole world. Why should we only ask Him to give us five or six people to lead to Christ when we could just as easily believe for hundreds, thousands, or even millions? This isn't to focus on "numbers" but to shatter the limitations we place on God. He's blessed me with the opportunity to see hundreds and hundreds of souls saved, and I'm just an ordinary person with no formal Bible training. I hope to be a part of many more amazing moves of God. Think about who it is we're talking about—*God*, the one who created it *all*.

> Something tells me He can handle our big prayers and that none of them are too massive for Him.

While I feel strongly about these and other dreams, I began to question the possibility that I had, perhaps, gone off the deep end. I needed to be reassured that I hadn't taken this faith thing "too far," as had been suggested. I wanted to know if visions and dreams as big as mine were as foolish as some thought, so I sought out godly counsel, the result of which was the following advice from a well-known pastor and author from the US. This is what he wrote to me:

First of all, God uses the person who has a dream, a vision, a goal. Nothing starts happening until somebody starts dreaming. Every accomplishment started off first as an idea in somebody's mind. If you aim at nothing, you are going to hit it.

Second, God uses the person who is willing to risk failure. When I moved here, I had no money, no members, no building, and I didn't know a single person. We had literally moved on faith because God said, "Go." It was an enormous risk. We had no guarantee that we were going to succeed, and there was no safety net beneath us. But God uses the person who is willing to risk failure.

Third, God uses the person who expects great things from God. You must be both realistic and optimistic. You must have high expectations. That is an evidence of faith. The difference between winners and losers is attitude. The person who says "I can" and the person who says "I can't" are both right. If you think you can't, believe me, you can't.

Finally, God uses the person who never gives up. God uses the person who is persistent, who is diligent, who doesn't know how to quit. The secret of success in the ministry is to just keep on keeping on. Outlast your critics. Great people are simply ordinary people who don't know how to quit. They don't know how to give up. Don't give up!

What a blessing and encouragement this was at a time when I had started to believe the skeptics. Thank God for the wisdom of those who have gone before! This is precisely why we share our stories—to build one another's faith.

We only get to do this life once, so let's make it count.

TRIALS AND TRIBULATIONS

Because it's a less travelled road, the faith walk is frequently misunderstood. For this reason, I'd like to address some of the stumbling blocks, barriers, and misconceptions I've encountered over the years, in the hopes of bringing clarity, understanding, and even revelation to that which often mystifies and confounds. One of the most common incorrect conclusions I've heard is that if the plan is of God, and the one called is "on track," then everything will go smoothly.

> People mistakenly believe that if God is in it,
> the road will be easy and breezy.
> Although a lovely thought, it's not a biblical one.

Often these same people think that if the one called experiences difficulty, then they have likely erred in some way. While this could be true for anyone at any time, it's interesting to note that throughout scripture, those listening intently to God, who had been asked to do or say something as directed by the Lord, rarely made it to their destinations without experiencing trouble. The truth is that the Christian faith walk isn't easy. So where does that leave us? Does this mean that trials and tribulations are a necessary part of the journey?

Well, in a word, yes. I say this with some degree of trepidation, recognizing that personal "religious" history will play a key role in how this response is viewed or understood. If you've been indoctrinated with the belief that God is sitting up in heaven with a great big stick, just waiting for you to make a mistake so He can hit you with it, then it will be difficult for you to comprehend the breadth and depth of God's love for you and His gift of forgiveness through Jesus Christ. You may also struggle with seeing God as a Father who loves you unconditionally if you've had an earthly father who was a less than stellar human being.

If that's you, then this next section is not directed at you but may still be of interest. The following thoughts are primarily intended for the consideration of those who are from backgrounds or churches that have simplified the Christian walk a little too much, having omitted the sections that deal with hardships.

I'm not trying to cause dissention in saying this, but neither of these extreme perspectives is fully correct. You can't talk about God and sin and not talk about God's mercy and grace. You also can't talk about faith and following Christ without talking about trials and tribulations that tend to come as part of the deal. Not long after I'd begun my walk of faith, I remember the comment of a friend who had been watching as I struggled with all the associated hardships: "If this is what living by faith looks like, then why would anyone ever want to do it?" I was stumped!

> The truth is, for most of us who have become so entangled by living "easy," a walk of faith that guarantees hardship is not very appealing.

Strangely, though, there are places around the world and eras of time in which the very decision to give your life to Christ, to fully live for Him, pretty much means or meant a death sentence. And not a simple death, but one of pain and torture. These people have a clear understanding of what it is to deny self, take up the cross, and lay down their lives for Christ. Let's consider this for a moment. Would you and I still choose Christ if we knew this would be the result?

I am such a huge fan of the love of God, sharing the love of God, and experiencing the love of God, but in truth, there's a side to the Christian walk that involves persecution and difficulties. I'm concerned that in our zeal to see people saved (I have an evangelistic heart myself) we may have simplified the walk a little too much. I know that we can't feed solids to a baby, but somehow even I, who had gone to church and small groups and Bible studies for most of my life, had missed this important detail.

Perhaps it was my own fault for not seeking the truth as fully as I should have, or maybe I was in denial that this part of the Word was as truthful as the love part. I really can't say for sure. However, one thing I can say for certain is that it's a pretty universal issue; otherwise, not only would I not have been so stunned by the harsh reality of what it took to stand with and for God, but neither would the church folk around me have been so appalled. It was because they found the whole premise so unattractive and foreign to what they "knew" that they ultimately rejected this life and discarded me.

Paul encouraged the church to hang on to their faith through these trials:

> *... no one should be shaken by these afflictions; for you yourselves know that we are appointed to this. For, in fact, we told you before when we were with you that we would suffer tribulation, just as it happened, and you know.* (1 Thessalonians 3:3–4)

Perhaps when people in the church see someone moving outside the norm, or even outside their own personal comfort zones, they allow worry, confusion, or anger to take hold of them. They assume that if a person begins to have trouble, they must be either sinning or off track somehow.

Although this is possible, what I'm talking about here is the faith walk, the obedient walk, the walk that has you living for Christ. If people are never taught that in living for Jesus trouble will come, then it stands to reason they will react poorly when hardship hits someone they already view as having "gone astray." They assume the trouble these folks are experiencing is because they are in error. Not so! As a word of encouragement to those who've overcome in spite of these obstacles, God's Word clearly states that those who are persecuted for righteousness' sake *will* be blessed!

Trouble is usually part of the deal.

It may sound as though I've been picking on the church or the believers, and I hope it doesn't, but here's why I'm saying what I'm saying. It's not to condemn but rather to encourage understanding. I hope that as a result of my sharing these experiences, others who choose this life, or whom God chooses for this life, will receive love and acceptance from within the body. You see, I fully expected to be persecuted by the world but was completely unprepared for the persecution that came from within the church. Call me naive, but I really thought believers would stand with me. Jesus said, "If the world hates you, you know that it hated me before it hated you," and "A servant is not greater than his master. If they persecuted me, they will also persecute you." Here's the key, though:

Scripture speaks of persecution coming from the world, not from the body. If it comes from the body, then it's on par with self-harming.

> Scripture speaks of persecution coming from the world, not from the body. If it comes from the body, then it's on par with self-harming.

This is most assuredly not God's way. As I travelled down this road of discovery, bewildered by what I was encountering, I found that I would receive pockets of support, but more often than not I was patronized, disregarded, judged, and in a number of cases, completely rejected by the body for living by faith. Why is that? I believe this happens because, as I said earlier, most aren't fully free of their "baggage."

This "stuff" that we've held on to can become cumbersome, greatly hindering our progress and our ability to work together. Sometimes people are jockeying for position or perhaps lashing out due to insecurities or jealousy. On other occasions it's about a sin that's clouding a person's vision, or simply because they don't like to see a faith walk that doesn't look like theirs. Whatever the reason, it's destructive and it slows a good work.

> Underlying or unresolved issues frequently rear their ugly heads when attempting to work together for God.

Sometimes a nasty spirit finds its way into a body of believers. This can also create problems. Obviously, it's not a good thing if there's resistance to the cause of Christ right *inside* the church. If we allow enemy strongholds into the church, we've obstructed both His blessings and our ability to effectively serve. I realize this isn't a popular notion, but the proof is in the fruit. If ugliness erupts from within the body, then something evil has been given a "right." Why else would we "blindly" hurt one another?

> Satan already has the world where he wants it; let's not give him the church too!

In humility, we need to bring our broken and fractured selves to Jesus for healing. We are all connected. We need one another. If we want to participate in the successful completion of God's plans, we need to be visibly different from the world. We must remain healthy in mind, body, soul, and spirit so that we can do our part amicably. After all, a house divided against itself falls.

I thought people were supposed to know we are Christians by our love. What happened to that? We need to love one another, even if we do things differently, see things differently, or look a little different from one another. If we don't love, we have become more like the world than like God. I don't want to get dragged down by those who are quick to point out the splinter in my eye, completely unaware of the tree in their own, nor do I wish for the reverse to occur.

> *"A new commandment I give to you,*
> *that you love one another;*
> *as I have loved you, that you also love one another."*
> (John 13:34)

That's a pretty tall order! He doesn't infer or suggest but actually commands us to love like He has. Notice the grammar; read the words after the semi-colon as one thought (*"as I have loved you, that you also love one another"*). We must love as He has. But Christ's love for us is completely sacrificial, unconditional, and absolutely never *self*-serving. How can we ever measure up to that? Well, we may not be able to, but He can, through us.

Our youngest daughter exuberantly jumped into the van along with her little buddy, talking a mile a minute about her upcoming birthday party plans. I was parked outside the elementary school, patiently waiting for the rest of the crew to emerge, when I overheard something being said about an invitation having gone to a boy completely unbeknownst to me. I felt a little exasperated, since I had spoken with her ahead of time about preparing her "invite" list prior to going to school so the numbers wouldn't get out of control. I was keenly aware she was well liked by many, but our financial resources were limited. I decided to wait and address it with her later, in private.

That evening I made another attempt to relate the guidelines for the party.

"Honey," I began, "remember how we'd spoken about the number of people you could invite to your party?"

"Yes." She nodded.

"Well, because you've already invited this boy, it means one of your other close friends won't be able to attend."

I reminded her of our previous conversation and the agreed upon number. She did recall and seemed to understand, but the sadness in her eyes broke my heart.

"Why did you invite this boy?" I asked.

"Well, Mommy," she began, "he isn't liked by anyone, and he's usually left out of things. He told me today that he has never been asked to a party before;

no one has ever invited him, so I asked him because I wanted him to feel loved and included."

My heart was in my throat. It was apparent that my _little_ girl had just taught me a _big_ lesson. Needless to say, her party guest list grew.

Let's hope that when our lives here on earth are over, we have died to self, living as He commanded and enabled, loving and sharing one another's burdens as we walk together on the narrow path He has set before us. Until that happens, we need to persevere through the barriers before us, refusing to allow criticism to discourage us or stop us from reaching our destiny, our calling. It can be a real kick in the gut when the cynics in our lives end up being the people or institutions we had admired. Actually, it hurts, and it's disappointing, but we need to shift that admiration over to God, with the understanding that He is the only one worthy of our praise and adoration. Although it can be painful, this shift toward dependency on God is a very good thing.

MISCONCEPTIONS

I recognize that a big deterrent to living by faith is a fear of lack, of not having enough and having to rely on God, who tends to operate in and through those around us. I really wish I didn't have to say this, but in all honesty, it _can_ be part of the price to pay. It doesn't always need to be this way, and it doesn't always remain this way, but it certainly _can_ be a part of the equation and, I might add, not a very pleasant part. That is, until you gain a deeper, fuller understanding. I am only now beginning to grasp some of these concepts, so while there may be holes, I'd like to share what I've learned thus far.

Receiving help in whatever form or fashion is humbling. Even when we understand the concept that _everything_ belongs to God, it's still difficult to acknowledge that there are occasions when we need to accept help from others. Why does "receiving" seem contrary to us? I think it's because we live in a culture that encourages and expects _self_-sufficiency.

What's interesting to note is that this sort of independence is in complete contradiction to how God operates.

> Jesus didn't do things independent of the Father or the Holy Spirit. Neither are we to act independently of Jesus.

Christ is the head and we are the body. We work together. If the head asks the arm and hand to pick something up and they don't, operations are slowed. If the foot moves but without instruction from the head, or in cooperation with the ankle, it can prove disastrous. We work as a team. If the eyes see danger but the body doesn't move to avoid it, then when ignored often enough, the eyes become weary of doing their job, and the body gets battered. We are warned to not become weary while serving, for in due season we will reap!

When *self*-reliant, we are separated from the body. I think that sometimes the reason for lack is to ensure that those of us who may appear to be, or who actually are, quite capable, clearly know that we are *unable* to do anything *alone*, ahead of, or separate from God's timing or plan! This is what happened, in part, to me. In order to avoid conflict and judgment, I had become quite independent. This autonomy was partially about creating a protective "barrier," but it was also the result of incorrect teaching.

I've also learned that the concept of giving-receiving-giving is an inescapable godly principle that's cyclical. We must give and we must receive. When we give, we're blessed with more to give, and when we receive, we can bless the giver not only by graciously receiving but also by praying for them.

I have a theory that when we have received, we are given a really significant window of opportunity to pray blessings on the giver that will be far more effective than if prayed by anyone else. So when you receive, make sure you pray for the one who gave. Ask them about their needs, pray, and then, God willing, see their prayers answered through you! In the end, we've all worked together and everyone gets blessed. The book of Acts tells us:

> *Now the multitude of those who believed were of one heart and one soul; neither did anyone say that any of the things he possessed was his own, but they had all things in common ... Nor was there anyone among them who lacked ... "* (Acts 4:32, 34a).

Why then, with all this giving and receiving, is there still lack? I think it's because we're not actualizing this strategy to its fullest, and in the case of many an individual, not at all. Of course, there are also bigger problems at play with our governments, our economic systems, and the ways in which our organized churches and charitable organizations are structured and how they distribute funds. Being self-reliant is somewhat rampant in our society and will take time to be reversed. I remember chatting with a dear, faithful friend about how in Western culture, a large portion of our lives is spent focused on growing our careers and accumulating "stuff." There's nothing wrong with stuff, and there's nothing wrong with working hard and achieving success. It's simply that a walk of faith, be it for a season or forever, is simply *not* about *self*.

If it were about getting ahead, then much of what God has required of us and of others would be quite ludicrous, unwise, and generally ridiculous. Quite to the contrary, though, the great part of all of this is that it's about *Him*, the Great I AM, the King of kings and the Lord of lords. The focus isn't on us and our accomplishments but on Him and His Kingdom work. The world tells us that dependency is equivalent to weakness, but it takes strength and courage of conviction to put all our trust and faith in Him. He is God, and we're not!

> We should have no confidence in the flesh
> but only in Christ.

Another misconception holds that faith is for lazy people, but faith isn't about slothfully sitting around, waiting for something to happen. Even those times when there's an expectation to rest in, or wait on, the

Lord, discipline and obedience in restraining oneself from rushing ahead of God is necessary. It still requires prayer and remaining focused on the goal. I could be wrong in this, but I have a funny feeling that the people God curtails are often those with a propensity for doing more than their part. It's the more sedentary individuals whom God may wish to encourage toward activity. The key point is that we are to do our part, no more, no less. This involves active listening, staying in the Word, seeking after and worshipping our Lord.

I think of "faith" as an action word.

Faith without works doesn't amount to much. If I believe there is a God but choose not to follow Him, then scripture says I'm no different than the demons. Believing, in and of itself, doesn't require work, for they (the demons) believe but do not follow. It's in the "following" that we are active and our faith comes alive! Following requires actually doing something. There are those who *do* many wonderful things, and although a blessing, this isn't faith either. We need faith *and* works. In order for faith to be alive, it must be acted upon. If I know that God wants me to bring His music to the world, but I don't actually do something as led, then it's a rather empty or dead kind of faith.

In order for the walls of Jericho to fall down, God required that His people march around the wall for seven days. They had to *do* something: "*But be doers of the word, and not hearers only, deceiving yourselves*" (James 1:22). Paul tells us to press toward the goal, to strive for the faith of the gospel, and to run the race before us. This sounds like something requiring effort. It doesn't seem passive, and it certainly doesn't seem like a pursuit one could achieve in a zombie-like state but rather the complete opposite. Pressing, striving, and running sound like action words. They even sound like work! Work like this requires a keen mind, energy, and passion.

Throughout the three years we brought music to the prison, we not only needed to be prepared musically, but there was quite a rigorous logistical procedure involved, including background inspections, criminal record checks, and orientation sessions. It was necessary for every volunteer at the prison to do this. When a member of our team was unable to attend, even just once, this meant the replacement would need to go through the entire process, which could take up to six weeks.

It was a race against time for each of our team members to get from their own church service and over to the prison on time. Sound gear, instruments, music stands, and more all needed to be loaded in and out of vehicles, onto dollies, and then taken through a number of secured doors. All of this took place before we'd even gotten to the room where the service would be held. Once there, we still needed to set everything up, sound check, and pray.

Yes, it was like a church plant, only different. It was different because most of our team members had already done this once that day at their own services, and now they were doing it again. It was also unique because of all the security measures and doors at the prison. We could only pass through one door at a time, so it was a lengthy process. I was blessed with a truly dedicated and passionate group. Although it was a cumbersome task and a hefty commitment, there was no groaning or complaining, only loyalty and faithfulness.

Serving and following are choices,
and they require effort.

Jesus did *not* say, "Join me. Life will be easy as we kick up our heels and then relax with a fruit drink on the beach." He said, *"... if anyone desires to come after Me, let him deny himself, and take up his cross daily, and follow Me"* (Luke 9:23). Oftentimes this means not going with the flow, not fitting in with the mainstream, and maybe even for a time not having nice things. Ouch! If that doesn't sound overly appealing to you, well, it didn't to me either.

What others don't realize about us "crazies" is that the choice wasn't to have trouble, create hardship for ourselves, upset our friends, or anything of the sort. That wasn't the choice we made, but it is a by-product associated with the commitment to deny ourselves and live for Christ. Although folks may fear for our sanity, I must assure and reassure them that we are quite lucid, certain, passionate, convinced, and convicted about that which we've been called to. What we'd love from those around us is prayer and whatever support they're led to offer.

From what I've read in the Bible, usually when Jesus forgave, healed, or delivered someone, it was as a result of *their* effort in seeking Him out, and then *His* grace and love poured out upon them. He asks us to seek and to knock. He requires that we give and serve, worship and pray, trust and obey.

We need to activate our faith by stepping into it, not by expecting it to suddenly come upon us.

A faith that is pure of heart sees us visiting orphans and widows who are troubled. These are activities that require effort, yet while we must be active, we're not justified by these works. We shouldn't expect our actions or good works to bring us into right relationship, as that would be based on law. We are justified solely by grace. Bottom line, though, a God-inspired "work" *will* activate our faith.

> *"For as the body without the spirit is dead, so faith without works is dead also."*
> (James 2:26)

Reflections

What biblical men/women/stories come to mind when considering faith in action?

How do you keep your faith alive when difficulties or conflicts arise?

How do we live God's way in this world?

SEVEN

Moving Forward in Faith

CALLING

Society tells us that we have the power within us to *have* or *do* anything we want, if we just put our minds to it. This is a worldly concept and not a godly one. In sharp contrast, God's Word says, "*I can do all things through Christ who strengthens me*" (Philippians 4:13). It's through Christ, not in and of ourselves, that we're able to do anything of lasting value. It's not about us or our self-created power! That is a lie of the enemy. It's all about God and His power. It's about the power of the Holy Spirit and the blood of Jesus; it's about the Trinity at work in and through us.

Even those who don't believe in God have received their gifts from Him. So even if the unsaved don't use their talents to glorify God, scripture says these gifts are from Him and are irrevocable! To move forward in faith, we must take our eyes off ourselves and fix them on Jesus.

> It's *not* about God bringing glory to us.
> It's about us bringing glory to God.

God is a jealous God. He wants all the credit and all the glory, not just the parts we decide to offer back, but *all* of it. Often people see Him as a God of rules and regulations, but He's a God of grace. That's why He sent His Son, Jesus, to obliterate legalism while effecting grace (where law would otherwise judge). This is where mercy triumphs over judgment (James 2:3). He looks at the heart and desires that true and lasting transformation take place.

We can't earn His blessings by what we do or even by who we are, but only by, and because of, Christ and His sacrifice. In our flesh, we sometimes like to revel in the spotlight, but He loves us too much to permit that for long. He saves us from ourselves because if we take the glory, then we have turned our accomplishments into idols. Idols aren't just gold and silver statues but anything that takes our focus off God and transfers it onto something else. This can even include that which we view as our own successes, possessions, careers, or talents, and it can happen to the most well-meaning individuals.

Picture the little old lady in the kitchen at church who becomes known for her cakes. In the beginning she bakes because she's gifted and wants to serve, but over time she finds herself seeking out and relishing the compliments of others, which begin to take a significant place in her heart, even to the point of giving her worth and "identity." By absorbing this identity, she begins to lose her true identity in Christ, thinking that it's the gift He gave her that gives her worth and position with God and people. But there isn't anything we can "do" to be made worthy. It's all about grace! God desires that we need Him and each other in order that His will be done. In working as a team, He is assured all the glory. This is one reason why unity is vitally important and why Satan is out to destroy unity within the body.

We're all wired to give. What's fascinating, though, is that the giving may look very different from one person to another. Some provide a listening ear, while others offer sound advice. Some lead, others follow, and although one might be called to "leave all" as led by God, another is called to finance that move.

> It's teamwork. It's Kingdom work, and it's God's way.
> One role is no more significant than another.

I would encourage you to seek the Lord in all things and at all times, expectant that He will hear your prayers and respond. Personally, I'd rather not rely on friends or leaders to provide me with answers, guidance, and revelation. While godly advisors are a blessing, I would prefer to go directly to the throne room of God.

> *"Let us therefore come boldly to the throne of grace,*
> *that we may obtain mercy and find grace*
> *to help in time of need."*
> —Hebrews 4:16

I believe that Jesus is my Lord and Saviour and I need only follow Him. Yes, I should honour those in authority here on the earth, knowing that their authority is given them by God, but first and foremost I must follow, serve, and receive direction from the Lord Himself.

There's a faulty teaching out there that says we will receive inspiration and instruction primarily through godly leaders rather than directly from God. Now, if we are referring to proven prophets who actually have had a word from the Lord that rings true in our spirits, then that's one thing. But I'm referring to something very different.

Over the years, it would seem that priests and pastors have been elevated to a position that is not entirely scriptural. As a result of this promotion, they have become our so-called connection to God. While the hearts of these men and women of God are typically pure, with a sincere desire to assist their flock in better hearing and knowing God, what seems to have occurred over time is unhealthy. We have asked them to perceive what the Lord is saying on our behalf rather than learning to hear from God ourselves. I don't wish to undermine these faithful servants who have committed their lives to shepherding the sheep, but rather to encourage the rest of us to broaden our perspectives and grow in the knowledge that we too have Kingdom authority.

It saddens me to think of the number of people who have missed out on executing a directive from God because it wasn't provided by, or confirmed through, a church leader. In giving others the power to determine our worthiness and calling, or to give us purpose and direction, we have both esteemed man and devalued God. That sounds harsh, but in truth, these leaders won't be with us on judgment day. We will stand alone before the Lord. In Galatians 1:10b, Paul says *"For if I still pleased men, I would not be a bondservant of Christ."*

Knowing Jesus in a uniquely intimate and personal way is the primary manner by which our faith grows. As we grow in relationship with Him, an unshakeable peace, revelation, and power of conviction comes into our hearts, based on that which we *know* to be true.

Nothing beats a certainty based on firsthand knowledge, wisdom, and assurance. After all, Jesus said,

> *"My sheep hear My voice, and I know them,*
> *and they follow Me."*
> (John 10:27)

God has frequently and historically asked people to do things that don't "fit" within the framework of the structure, program, or mandate of pre-existing organizations. Our Christian culture can limit us by dictating that whatever God requires of us must line up with an already established umbrella organization under which it should be covered, ordained, or blessed.

> Under what banner did the disciples operate?
> What about Moses?
> How does the call on Esther's life fit with this theory?
> These people all operated under the banner of the Lord!

I'm not against serving in a godly organization, and I also believe that prayer support and accountability in ministry is vital. However, God is doing a new thing, and therefore the old wineskin—the old ways—simply won't work. If we dig in our heels and maintain the expectation that each call or work must match up with something that's already been deemed worthy, then we're in for a big surprise.

This mindset is hugely restrictive. It took me a long while to look at this with new eyes, and I had to undergo a major paradigm shift. But once I did, this deep and undeniable revelation brought incredible peace and freedom! How wonderful it is to know that I am fully, completely, and directly under the great I Am.

This shift in thought may take some time to process, so start by trying to think of it in a different way. If you as a parent instruct your child to wash the dishes, you expect they will comply and follow the task through to its completion. It would be laughable for that child to later approach a sibling and ask for a second opinion, especially when they'd already heard from you, the highest authority on the issue.

Although this may sound silly, the concept isn't. God must shake His head in bewilderment each time we question the validity of His request by checking it with other people. While receiving a second witness is extremely important, we do need to be cautious as to where, and in whom, we put our trust. I've found the most effective confirmation usually comes via a vessel chosen by God, not a perspective or person selected by us.

Having come to this revolutionary understanding, I made another startling discovery that complicates matters further. I came to the realization that some pastors were never actually called to be pastors. Now, before jumping to a position of defence, allow me to explain what I mean by this. Here's what I believe may have happened. Over time, when a person felt called into ministry, they were funnelled into the role of pastor, priest, or missionary. The position of a minister is, generally speaking, the most secure and conventional, while that of the missionary is familiar but requires more effort and provides less stability.

Here's what I'm wondering.

> Where is the place, job, or support for the prophet, the
> apostle, the teacher, or the evangelist if they don't
> choose to become a pastor?

How many of those who are anointed in these areas slid into the role of pastor out of necessity? It's understandable if this was the only outlet for ministry, work, or a job. But this would mean that many of those currently in the role of pastor were never actually meant to be pastors. Our culture has structured the church in such a way that most of the funding is based around the role of pastor, a position mentioned only a couple of times in all of scripture. Appropriate allowance has not been afforded the other roles. Not only that, but pastors are expected to carry out a number of obligations that are likely well outside their gifting, calling, and anointing.

Conversely, others who have remained confident in their calling, convinced God was asking them to assume the role of prophet, apostle, evangelist, or teacher, inevitably had nowhere to go because they didn't fit within the existing parameters, nor did they feel led to the local church. Many of these felt unable to carry out the call on their lives. How sad!

This means that we have a number of discouraged pastors who were never called to be pastors but have been charged with a role they aren't equipped to fill. We have frustrated prophets, apostles, evangelists, and teachers who have not realized their calling because there has been no place for them, causing them to move into unsuitable positions or to actually walk out their calling but without support. And then there is another misunderstood group, called pioneers.

It had been a wildly eventful few days and weeks leading up to our very first outdoor gospel music festival. It was a huge undertaking. The team had, literally, built everything from the ground up. It was a scorching hot day, and the first act had just hit the stage when I experienced a wave of intercession that was unlike anything I'd undergone before or after. I began sobbing uncontrollably, and it felt as though I was in a cloud of some sort and quite unaware of my surroundings. This event lasted for at least half an hour.

As this experience was coming to a close, I got called away to do a TV interview. You can only imagine the mess I was in at that point. As I darted off to fix my face, the artist who had been on stage during most of this stopped me and said, quite out of the blue, "You do know you're a prophetic apostle, right?" I actually don't even know how I responded, but I did not know that.

As the years went on, the truth of this statement was confirmed. I never really felt prophetic, but I grew to understand that I was living and experiencing things before other people did. I was, and am, a pioneer. What revelation! I don't think I'd ever fully understood how people viewed my life until one day a well-meaning friend asked, "Do you feel as though things have just never taken off for you?" I was speechless. I actually felt the complete opposite—that thanks to God, I'd been able to accomplish a great deal for the Kingdom. It was then I understood. Ahhhhh! If you start something but don't do it forever, you aren't considered successful. Well, this isn't how it works for pioneers. We start lots of things, as led by the Lord, so that once initiated (and the fields have been ploughed), others can take up the mantle more easily.

Pioneering brings with it an unsubstantiated chastisement that we are a group of wild and undisciplined lone rangers. This perspective comes from a lack of understanding. Five, ten, or twenty years down the road, none of what we've done looks strange anymore and might even be commonplace. A friend once spoke this over me: "You have a global mandate, putting aside everything that so easily entangles, being in the world, but not of it, pioneering in difficult places. Not every stake will work because the ground won't receive it at first, but there will be success in the end. You will complete the work you were created to complete."

> Even Jesus was seldom acknowledged as the Saviour,
> Healer, Redeemer, and King that He was and is,
> because of people's preconceived notions of
> how a king should look or act.

Jesus didn't present Himself as royalty, and people often didn't recognize His authority, but that doesn't change the fact that He was and is the King of kings and the Lord of lords. He simply walked in, and with an authority given Him by His Father, all while being a servant to all. He knew His call and destiny, and He completed His mandate. In God's realm, the last is first and the first, last.

To be great in God's kingdom, we must serve. To gain life, we must lose it. His ways are not ours. It's all flipped upside down! As one who is committed to a life of faith, I desire to be true to the call on my life, even if it means going against the norm.

For those who hurl accusations, presuming that this group sees itself as "better," I am aghast. I can't imagine seeing myself as being above anyone.

The very thought that one person would see themselves as more valuable than another is a scary slippery slope! I don't think it would take God long to shut this down with a few sharp reminders of what it took to get us to where we are. I think He'd cause us to recall the fiery furnace of trials and testing He used to refine us and bring us to a place of complete surrender. And how once we were in this broken, helpless, contrite state, He was at long last able to use us for His purposes.

I actually went through a time of suffering that left me feeling beaten down to the place of paralysis. While in this mind-set, I came very close to losing my identity in Christ. This is not a good place to be. Feeling that badly about ourselves can become a huge stumbling block to God being able to use us. Satan will hang on tightly to self-hatred and will feed it with all things unhealthy. While dying to self is a prerequisite to the faith, we should balance this with knowing who we are in Christ and who Christ is in us.

> We need to remain steadfast, knowing we are sanctified, redeemed, and bought with an incredible price.

We ought to be filled with the truth of how God sees us, assured that even when we're in error, He loves us. When we repent, requesting God's forgiveness through His Son, Jesus, not only does He forgive us, but He wipes the slate clean. He has no memory of our sin. Satan, however, has a very long and evil memory. He wants to ensure that we not forget our mistakes. When we're wrapped up in guilt, despair, and self-condemnation, we're of little use to God, and that's just how Satan likes it! Don't allow Satan's lies to infiltrate your mind or spirit.

We need to grab hold of the freedom that's ours in Christ! It's meant for all of us, not just some of us. When living for Him, we are *all* chosen, adopted, joint heirs with Christ, justified, righteous, sanctified, redeemed, accepted, healed, and deeply loved, which makes us *all* His favourites! Galatians 2:6 says, "*God shows personal favouritism to no man …*"

Whenever possible, speak out the truths of God, and don't receive the lies of the enemy. Let's continually remind ourselves of who we are and whom we serve. Our roles have no bearing on how deeply He loves us. Just because one child is asked to take out the trash, and the other to set the table doesn't put one above the other. Again, we are the body of Christ, and each part is integral and important. An ear cannot be an eye and shouldn't try.

> Those called to a task with heavy responsibility are
> usually humbled and feel ill-equipped
> to serve in their callings.

Regardless of how inadequate one feels, obedience is expected. I've noticed that those who observe our walk tend to focus on either the highs (the cool moves of God, the miracles, the "wow!" factor) or the lows (moving against the flow, experiencing hardship, the minimalistic lifestyle). Being an optimist, I tend toward concentrating on the good elements, but both exist. In order to experience and see God in a heightened form, there will be sacrifice, pain, and suffering involved. In our flesh, we only want the highs.

> He gives us a choice as to whether or not we will drink
> of the cup given us.

Even Jesus struggled when He begged of the Father, prior to his crucifixion, *"if it is possible, let this cup pass from Me"* (Matthew 26:39a). Of course, He also said, *"nevertheless, not as I will, but as You will"* (Matthew 26:39b). None of us desire the difficult days, but they are part of the journey. No one grows on the mountaintop but in the valley, and as a result of the climb, we are stretched and bettered.

LIFE ON THE EDGE

Our final week in Canada was upon us. It was strange to think we were leaving our home and native land behind. We were confident we'd be back to visit but had no idea if we'd ever live in Canada again. It was bittersweet. Before we knew it, we were packed: five people, fifteen pieces of luggage, passports and visas in hand, all set for our adventure, armed with little more than our Bibles, God's promises, and the prayers of those who were standing with us! We were blessed to spend time with my parents at the airport prior to leaving the country. It was wonderful to see them and to know that they were blessing us as we went.

As I embraced my mom and dad at the gate, I could see the tremendous look of loving parental pride on their faces. They had always been incredibly supportive, and this time was no different.

Today, though, I saw something particularly touching in my dad's eyes. It was an immense sadness coupled with an undeniable love for his family. He looked at us with those warm blue eyes as his only daughter, her husband, and these three beloved grandchildren were about to embark on yet another phase of this journey with God. He was proud but also heartbroken to see us go, and he bore the countenance of a man who clearly thought he'd never see us again.

I tried to remain positive, wrestling with my emotions, all the while attempting to stay focused on the mission at hand. And so with smiles on our faces and clouded vision, we hugged as they blessed us and bravely wished us well. We waved, blew kisses, and walked through the gate.

To say that it was easy to leave everything and everyone we knew behind would be untruthful. Essentially, our entire history, both the good and the bad, was being left in this land, while our future, a complete mystery to us, was before us in a new country. Though difficult to comprehend, we were greatly encouraged by Jesus' words:

> *… Assuredly, I say to you, there is no one who has left house or parents or brothers or wife or children, for the sake of the kingdom of God, who shall not receive many times*

> *more in this present time, and in the age to come everlasting life.* (Luke 18:29–30)

This verse provided us with a sense of hope and expectancy as we ventured into the unknown. I realize that speaking of the "unknown" in this way must sound more like a line from a *Star Trek* episode than a truthful word spoken by a person of faith, but we were stepping into uncharted territory. "*For we walk by faith, not by sight*" (2 Corinthians 5:7). To walk by faith, we must be willing to undertake that which is unfamiliar, trusting that God is not only leading us but holding us by the hand, gently and purposefully guiding us every step of the way.

My personal faith walk seems to have changed and progressed over time, and while it's not typical or predictable, it's not particularly puzzling either. What I found fascinating about the process God took us through in preparation for our time in Scotland was the consistency in how He spoke and in what He expected. He would provide a word like "get passports" or "get luggage" or whatever it happened to be. We would do as told, and only after we had obeyed would we receive confirmation.

When we purchased our luggage, we discovered that it was the last day of a sale in a town with very few options in the way of department stores. If we hadn't obeyed at the time He'd spoken, we still would have gotten the luggage, but the cost would have been significantly higher, and our options would have been limited. In the case of the passports, we were unable to be instantly obedient because of a very real barrier—a lack of funds. So we committed it to prayer, and He provided within twenty-four hours. This allowed us the means to move forward, which we did, without delay.

Confirmations *only* came *after* we had been obedient. Even in the case of making the decision to ship our belongings to Inverness, it was only *after* we had called the shipping company and committed to the destination that the confirmation of the location came. Again, it was imperative that we hear and act in obedience, and then we would receive confirmation.

> Early in our walk, we would have required a number of
> confirmations prior to stepping out to do anything,
> but as time passed, this all changed.

Not only did the confirmations *not* come until after we had obeyed, but more often than not, we were also given *no* further instructions until we had done what had been asked of us. We needed to trust that we could "hear," and He needed to trust that we would obey. So much of what I see in the Christian community is contrary to faith. I hear people say things like, "God said I'm to leave my job right away, but I'm not going to do that until I have something else." If my husband and I had used that logic (and it is logical), we wouldn't have experienced Scotland, because there never was a "job" in the worldly sense. Those who view our actions in the natural say that these decisions make us reckless and unwise. To be honest, in the natural it does appear fairly irresponsible, but when looking at it through spiritual eyes, it's not.

What's the difference between living by faith and being reckless? Were the disciples too hasty when they dropped everything to follow Jesus? What about Jonah? He hesitated and ran in the opposite direction, causing hardship and delay. God gave Jonah an opportunity to repent, whereas Lot's wife disobeyed and, within the blink of an eye, became a pillar of salt. I'd rather not test God's patience any more than I already have.

> If I've made a commitment to follow God, then I'm
> going to follow God.

It's not about how good it feels, comfortable it is, or how it looks to others. It's about fully embracing the Christian walk of faith, because that's what's required of me! I've often heard people say that God won't give us more than we can handle. This is *not* true. Of course He will! He gives us more than we can handle so that we will draw closer to Him and He can handle it for us. This way, He receives the glory. First Corinthians 10:13 is frequently misquoted, as it speaks of "temptations," not hardships! Bottom line, He is worthy of our praise, and we can trust Him. There are lots of ups and downs, but it's tremendously exhilarating to walk hand-in-hand with the King.

PRESSED, NOT CRUSHED

I wish I could report a journey of smooth sailing, but alas, what we experienced was more accurately a rocky and stormy ordeal! We wrongly assumed that because preparations in Canada had been so easy (a high), the entire process would be effortless—*not*! This is when the reality of it being God's plan and not ours was clearly evident.

Upon our arrival in Scotland, we were confronted with a substantial "low" as we faced the bleak and startling reality that there was absolutely *nothing*, from a worldly perspective, in place. There was no one to greet us. There was no one to show us around. There was no one to help us get oriented. There was no one to teach us the Scottish ways.

We were completely and totally at the mercy of God.

Obviously, this is *not* a bad place to be, but trusting God at such a deep level from such a seemingly helpless state of being was beyond uncomfortable. We encountered a number of challenges right from the get go. Once we'd collected our belongings, we needed to find a vehicle to transport us to the B & B. Given that automobiles are smaller in the UK (I guess most people only have one or two children), this dilemma turned out to be an ongoing obstacle throughout our entire time in Scotland. However, on this particular day, we not only needed to move five people, but also a *lot* of luggage.

Once we'd sorted out the transportation challenges, we discovered that because the houses are also smaller than what we were accustomed to, there wasn't even enough room for all our suitcases at the B & B. We were also stunned to discover that our accommodation had no internet connection, nor did it have a telephone. This was 2007 so most facilities still had landlines and we did not have a cell phone yet! Everything was different, from driving on the opposite side of the road, to terminology, to systems and technology, to absolutely everything. We'd only just arrived and were already experiencing more of a culture shock than anticipated. At least we spoke the same language, sort of!

We barely understood a word they said, but that was apparently part of the fun!

The first few days in Inverness were challenging and stressful, and the task before us daunting. It was difficult to find a frame of reference, because everything was so different. We needed to find a neighbourhood in which to live, a home, a school, jobs, a bank, a place of worship, and more. We were overwhelmed.

Our home base turned out to be of no real use to us because the B & B where we were staying was locked up throughout the day. This meant the five of us meandered (mostly on foot) throughout the city for hours at a time, each and every day for fourteen days.

The first thing we noticed on these ridiculously long days was the incredible spiritual oppression. It was thick. This is the only way I can describe the experience or sensation. From the very first day that we began to orient ourselves in the town centre, we knew we needed to be outfitted in our spiritual armour and immediately began to pray for the city and the country, believing that God's desire was to heal and bless this land. We boldly asked that with every step we took, God would break off that which bound many of these people in a somewhat depressive state, something I'll speak more about later.

We decided to launch our Scottish adventure by searching for a good school. It made sense that our first stop be the school board. Unfortunately, this was of no help. What we did learn was that not only were our kids later to start than anticipated, but many of the schools were already full and didn't accept new students. We inquired as to which schools did have availability, only to be told that it was our responsibility to find out for ourselves! This meant we needed to call or visit each institution to see if they would accept our kids. In a daze, the five of us set out once again, wandering the city streets and investigating schools, without a vehicle, a phone, or a computer.

> This lack of "customer service" was just one of the many occasions in which we were reminded that we were no longer in Kansas … I mean Canada!

The only redeeming aspect associated with all this running around was that we were familiarizing ourselves with the city! There didn't appear to be any internet cafes, so we were ecstatic when we stumbled upon some computers at the library. Whew! While they limited our time on them, at least we were able to let our friends and family know that we were safe.

In a valiant attempt to use our allotment of computer time wisely, we also tried to investigate the Inverness housing situation. We were shocked to find that rentals were double the price we had paid in Canada *and* one also had to pay council taxes *and* these very same houses were less than half the size! We also learned that one could not rent a home without having a bank account.

Armed with that crucial piece of information, we headed off to the bank to get an account. This is where things went from bad went to worse. They informed us that one cannot get a bank account without an address! What? To reiterate, we couldn't get a house without a job or a bank account and we couldn't get a bank account without an address!

On top of all that, the banks wouldn't take our traveller's cheques. We had no credit cards and were faced with the distressing news that the Canadian dollar was at a value of less than half the British pound. In essence, with one swift move, we had just lost more than half our money, and we didn't have a lot to begin with!

This is more significant than it sounds because the ramifications of this discovery were that rather than the anticipated six months to get settled, we could only afford three! After that, we would have no money! It was becoming next to impossible to find a silver lining. We decided to look for jobs. This would require getting a National Insurance Number (similar to a SIN or an SSN). After setting out to do this, we were told that we needed to prove that we had applied for jobs *before* they would give us the card. Strangely, we were unable to fill out on-line job applications without a NIN! Again, to clarify, we needed a National Insurance

Number in order to apply for a job, but we couldn't apply for work without a National Insurance Number!

Yes, we were shaking our heads too! I'd never heard of anything so absurd. It was discouraging beyond words, and I felt as though I'd entered the twilight zone. We had no choice but to keep moving. If we believed the "theology" that if God was in it, all would go smoothly, this would have been a mistake of gargantuan proportions.

After fourteen gruelling hours of walking from one school to another, to housing offices and potential "lets" (rental property locations), along with a number of other stops along the way, I looked over at my kids, astounded. This was day three, and they hadn't complained ... at all! Personally, I could feel myself losing a grip on what little remained of my positive attitude, yet here were my kids, all of who were at an age and stage when this entire experience could have been viewed as disastrous, and they were persevering through the trials like real troopers.

Gratitude swelled up inside of me, and the tears were difficult to contain. I could feel tremendous pressure on my chest as the burden before us seemed insurmountable. Had we made a mistake? Was it supposed to be this difficult? I was desperate to understand and fraught with discouragement. It was the steady and unwavering attitude of my teens that motivated me and strengthened my resolve to carry on.

When we next accessed a computer, I received an email that shattered my heart. It carried with it the news that my dad had been diagnosed with metastatic amelanotic melanoma. Cancer. We were stunned, disheartened, and growing increasingly weary of the obstacles before us and the effort it was taking to disallow depression and heartache from overtaking us. We were absolutely in a "low," having found ourselves not simply on the mission field, something we were somewhat prepared to face, but also on the battlefield with very few reinforcements and not a big arsenal at our disposal. Those initial days felt like a nightmare. The battle was on!

Reflections

When you're in the valley, how do you find comfort in knowing who you are in Christ?

What brings you life? What inspires and excites you?

Have your gifts and callings found a place or a community in which they (you) can thrive?

EIGHT
STRATEGIES IN FAITH

VICTORY IN BATTLE

Although I've mentioned the challenges associated with spiritual warfare, I haven't really delved into it much, mostly because this is both a sensitive and a very big subject. But I would be remiss if I didn't address the reality of what it means to operate while under serious opposition.

We Christians have an enemy, and his name is Satan. While we serve a God who wants to save us, set us free, love us, forgive us, and provide us with everlasting life, the enemy wants nothing more than to discourage us, defeat us, divide us, and destroy us. If we wander out onto the battlefield completely unaware, we are on dangerous ground. As you read, I'd ask that your ears be opened to the reality of my experience and that you suspend preconceived beliefs, teachings, or judgments in order to better hear how the Lord faithfully directed me.

Initially when producing the concerts, I unwittingly moved upon the enemy camp, quite unaware of the ramifications of having performed such an act. While it's right and good to go into the world, remember that just as soldiers don't go to war without a strategy and an understanding of their enemy, neither should we.

So when you go, be prepared!
Warfare is a very real part of the faith journey.

When Christians keep to themselves, they aren't a significant threat to the enemy, yet Satan is still known to instigate strife and division whenever possible. However, the heat really gets turned up when we, with Christ in us, infiltrate the world, a place Satan sees as his territory. At this point, the enemy is incredulous at the apparent audacity of our actions, motivating him to pull out all the stops to prevent further godly activity. We needn't allow ourselves to be scared off by this, but we also shouldn't diminish the reality of the situation.

> *"Be sober, be vigilant; because your adversary the devil walks about like a roaring lion, seeking whom he may devour."*
> (1 Peter 5:8)

Note that this scripture says *"may"* devour. Satan needs our permission to do this (unless the issue is unconfessed sin or a failure to trust in Christ alone). If we stand fast, well-equipped with knowledge and understanding, confident that we live in victory with Christ, whose very name causes the enemy to quiver in fear and flee, we'll know the security and peace that we have in Him. That's incredibly good news! We are instructed to submit to God, resist the devil, and then live with the assurance that he will leave us alone. We as believers have authority in Jesus' name over the devil. Jesus, who reigns in us, is far more powerful than the enemy. Once we recognize our delegated authority and effectively use that authority, we will be in a very good position to go into battle. The following verse is critical to understanding that authority:

> *"Behold, I give you the authority to trample on serpents and Scorpions, and over all the power of the enemy, and nothing shall by any means hurt you."*
> (Luke 10:19)

That is powerful! It says that "nothing" will hurt us! How comforting to know that even in the midst of trials, the battle has already been won. We who are in Christ are on the winning team. We've been given a sneak peek at the scoreboard, and we win hands down!

Throughout our years in the Canadian Rockies, most of our time was spent in a provincial park where wildlife was free to roam. We were accustomed to this, so I felt comfortable going for walks on my own through wooded areas. On one such trek, I was deep in thought when the Holy Spirit prompted me to make some noise by clapping my hands. As I did this, I came around the bend only to see that I had startled, just a few feet in front of me, a bear—a large bear. In fact, it was a full-grown grizzly. We were used to being surrounded by elk, deer, the occasional moose, and a number of black bears, but never before had we encountered a grizzly. Although my heart skipped a beat, I was remarkably calm.

Slowly backing away, I remembered what I'd learned from a documentary, which was to talk and wave my arms as a signal to this poor-sighted animal that I was a person and not a predator. As I was doing this, I realized that the words I had spoken were words of spiritual authority: "I have dominion over you, in Jesus' name, and you don't want me!" The bear went his way and I went mine. Well, actually, I went in the opposite direction. I have faith, but I don't have a death wish!

> I'm convinced that there are many occasions when trouble comes and all we need to do is take authority.

Prior to one of the concerts, we were having some fairly significant issues with the theatre's high-end sound gear. None of the professional technicians could sort out the problem. Frustrated, they decided it might be a blown fuse. Moments after I left the theatre to find a replacement fuse, I prayed a prayer of authority, binding the enemy from touching the gear. Almost immediately after praying, my cell phone rang. It was the technicians advising me that I could return because the gear was, "for some unknown reason," working again!

Another example was the day we were setting up for our outdoor gospel music festival. One of the members of our team was made aware of a woman, unknown to us, who was making her way around the grounds. As it turned out, she was a witch who was there on a mission of her own. She was as determined as we were to see change, but with a very different outcome in mind. We gathered together and prayed with the victory that we knew was ours until she left. In the spirit, one member, who wasn't on site at the time, had "seen" her leave something behind. He told us not to worry, that God was going to deal with it Himself. So, having done our part, we trusted Him to do His.

At the event the following day, there were so many miraculous activities that I had completely forgotten about the witch. What's fascinating is that God hadn't forgotten His promise, and while our group was worshipping on the stage, He took care of what the she had left. It was a very hot day with absolutely no breeze until the moment that a focused heavenly wind passed directly over the stage and through our banner, which was attached to the roof of the stage. The wind blew the banner from one end to the other and over to a place on the ground beside the stage, where these white wings, for want of a better word, touched down and then lifted again. It was the very place where the witch had left her ill-intentioned gift. The Lord used what was intended for evil to bless us! Of course, the crowd that was gathered gasped with awe and reverence.

> *"But thanks be to God, who gives us the victory through our Lord Jesus Christ."*
> (1 Corinthians 15:57)

We are given a strategy to handle ourselves in the battle. There are many good books on this subject that I would encourage you to read, but for now, at the very least, be certain to put on your armour every day as outlined in Ephesians 6:11–17: *"Put on the whole armor of God, that you may be able to stand against the wiles of the devil"* (v. 11). Alert the heavenlies aloud each and every day as to whom you serve. Let there be no doubt that you are under the power, authority, and jurisdiction of Jesus Christ.

I'd like to share a truly freeing perspective that I hope will encourage you as it did me. A friend of mine was preaching one day and spoke about not only knowing one's enemy but also how crucial it is to know one's own army! I thought this was very insightful. While there are Christians who don't want to acknowledge that the devil exists, there are others who are more familiar with demons than they are with angels. I find this to be rather peculiar.

> Scripture clearly indicates that
> both demons and angels exist.

In having a deeper understanding of the army that stands with and for us, our fortitude to walk in faith is strengthened. I would encourage you to gain a greater understanding of the spiritual realm, or that which is supernatural. This isn't new-fangled mumbo jumbo. This is scriptural.

Many people in the Bible received visitations from angels. We're told that in the end times, God will pour out His Spirit on all flesh. Dreams and visions will occur more frequently and, I might add, they already are, which means exactly what it sounds like it means! Time is short. The supernatural realm of heaven is merging with the natural as His Kingdom comes to earth. This is why, with each passing day, there's more talk of the supernatural in the world and in the Church. Ask God for wisdom in this so that you might easily discern the work of the enemy from the work of the Lord.

If you've hit a formidable wall in your battle and nothing seems able to knock that thing down, keep in mind that it may not have been put there by Satan. God can also create barriers, but they are constructed for good, to teach us something or to preserve His timing.

If you take authority and it doesn't seem to be "working," either persevere, request the prayers and assistance of friends and spiritual leaders, fast, or when all else fails, trust that it's God's will, God's "wall," and it's in His hands. The Lord is sovereign. He will create calamity and harden hearts to suit His plans and purposes. There's no real formula for knowing if it's Him or not, other than knowing Him, growing in the Spirit, in the Word, and in prayer.

We all need to work through those times when we're unsure and must determine whether we are to wait on the Lord or push through the difficulty. Pray that your eyes and ears be opened to the leading of the Holy Spirit. Faith is like a muscle, and the only way to grow that muscle is by battling through the resistance.

> Without resistance or trouble,
> our faith would never grow!

PUSHING THROUGH

During those initial days in Scotland, I felt despondent and beleaguered. One evening as I sat on our bed at the B & B re-hashing the situation in my mind, our son unexpectedly appeared at the door, Bible in hand. Being a quiet, introspective, and unassuming young man, it was remarkable to me that he had willingly come to us with both scripture and insight. I think I was as stunned as I was encouraged by the obvious growth. His words and heart inspired me to carry on, despite the oppression that threatened to consume me. Although there were many more obstacles with which to deal, and a multitude of emotions to control (too many to list), we kept on plodding through the muck and mire.

I decided to email a trusted friend, coveting her prayers, knowing that we were absolutely in need of breakthrough. She had a dream that very night in which we were all surrounded by a very frightening tornado! It was racing toward us, and we were all running as fast as our legs would take us. She yelled for us to get down and then threw her body over ours to protect us. When she woke up, the Lord told her that's precisely what she was to do—cover us in love, prayer, and support.

Our family had arrived in this country purposefully and rightfully, with ancestral ties and in accordance with God's wishes, and the enemy was not happy. This had apparently kicked up some serious spiritual dust—dust of tornado-sized proportions! So with that, my dear friend enlisted others to pray and fast with her.

> *... for assuredly, I say to you, if you have faith as a mustard seed, you will say to this mountain, "Move from here to there," and it will move; and nothing will be impossible for you. However, this kind does not go out except by prayer and fasting.* (Matthew 17:20b–21)

I am delighted to say that it was soon after their act of obedience that mountains began to move! The Lord led us to the district of Culloden/

West Hill, and it was here, in this very region, that we finally found a great school and miraculously, still without a bank account, we found our home. Breakthrough! We were elated and deeply grateful.

"The only way to secure a rental home without a bank account would be to deal directly with the home owner." This was the firm response from the letting agency. With that piece of information, our options had dwindled substantially. The house we were about to go and see, like the majority of homes we'd found, was in the hands of a solicitor. Kevin and I seriously doubted whether it was worth the time and cab fare to go and take a look.

As we discussed the possibility of not making the trip, our son piped up with, "I think we should go and see the house, because you never know what God might do!" We were stunned by both his faith and his wisdom. We agreed, ordered a cab, and off we went. The house was tiny and clean and in the correct catchment area for our school of choice. Surprisingly, the owner himself happened to be present at the time of viewing, so we were able to meet him in person and even have a brief conversation before the next family to see the house arrived.

Nothing transpired until a week later, after all this prayer and fasting had occurred. The solicitor's office called and told us that the homeowner wanted to speak with us directly. I called him back, and he asked why we hadn't rented his home. I told him of our predicament. He said, "I really don't know why, but I feel compelled to help you." He wanted to rent us his home, regardless of the rulings from the solicitor's office! Not only that, but he knocked fifty pounds off the monthly rent, too! Not only was this offer completely remarkable, but because houses were being rented the very day they'd been advertised, it was truly miraculous that God had held the house for us for more than a week!

At long last we had a home in Scotland. We were ecstatic until we realized that we had one teensy weensy little problem. Our container of belongings, which had been delayed, was originally a blessing but now a hindrance.

We didn't have anything with which to live: no plates or cutlery, no mats, blankets or pillows … nothing!

Well, wouldn't you know it, after having attended just two different churches, once each, folks started showing up at our very empty house with things for us to use until our personal effects arrived! Praise God! We felt so blessed. Finally, with a rental agreement in hand, we could also acquire a bank account, or so we thought. Unfortunately, this didn't actually take place for yet another six weeks. Thank the Lord that some of our friends from Canada began to wire us money for groceries, or things would have been far worse.

God was definitely with us, but some days I struggled with my desire to go back home. It's challenging to put into words; it felt as though I needed to run away, far away, as quickly as my short little legs would allow, or else my heart would explode from the pain and discomfort. It literally took everything I had, and then some, to remain calm and not act on this anxiety. It was after one such occasion that God presented me with some pretty major correction when He lovingly but firmly led me to Luke 9:62, which says,

"But Jesus said to him, 'No one, having put his hand to the plow, and looking back, is fit for the kingdom of God.'"

Ouch! That was sobering and stayed with me. Strangely enough, just a few lines after that scripture is one that we encountered on a number of occasions after arriving in the UK. It speaks of the need for labourers. Given that there had been a desperate plea for labourers in Scotland, we were puzzled by the resistance and suspicious nature that greeted us.

The people of Scotland are lovely and friendly, so their suspicion wasn't anything overt but rather something unspoken. It occurred to me that God had responded to their prayers, sending quite a number of labourers, and they (we) had responded, coming from Canada, the US, Australia, Switzerland, Holland, Ireland, England, Wales, South Africa, and Poland, to name just a few!

> I think that when these beautiful, humble Scottish people prayed, what they wanted were labourers from Scotland, but instead they got us.
> We weren't quite what they had in mind.

It just goes to show the truth in that old adage, "Be careful what you pray for!" Although we were feeling somewhat displaced and a little off balance in our new environment, we were also being given an unbelievable number of opportunities to share our faith. So in pushing through and past the pain and anxiety, I kept my eyes fixed on the Lord and the task before me.

After hearing our "accents," the number one question was always the same: "Where are you from?" This would be followed by a puzzled, "Why would you move here?" Many of those we met couldn't understand why we'd left Canada. The non-believers in particular described their lives and circumstances as being quite abysmal and regularly spoke to us of their desire to leave the area.

At first this seemed strange, considering the beauty of the landscape—the ocean, the mountains, and the rich and honoured heritage. It also didn't jibe with the statistics that clearly stated Inverness was the fastest growing community in all of Europe. So in the natural, this seemed very odd, but in the spiritual, it really wasn't strange at all, especially knowing and sensing firsthand the spiritual heaviness that was there.

It didn't take long to discover how this dark atmosphere had come to be. As we gained a deeper understanding of Inverness and its history, the battle of Culloden and the disturbing amount of high-level witchcraft present, it was clearly evident that this darkness had built up over many years. Curses had come upon this place as a result of generational sin, bloodshed, and rampant demonic, druid, and cult activity. It was alarming to note that much of this was accepted as normal and considered "part of the culture," likely because it had been this way for so long.

Although it was a little uncomfortable responding to ongoing questions about our move from every person we met, we also recognized it had been meticulously and wonderfully designed to be precisely as it was. It would have been far simpler to share reports of a fantastic new job or of a family member who had inspired this move, but that was not God's plan.

When asked by everyone from cab drivers and shopkeepers to the school's staff and potential employers as to why we had moved, all we could say was "God led us here." Even if we attempted to give our answers a more palpable twist, we'd have had no way of backing them up. So for the time being, nice, light conversations had become a thing of the past!

> These experiences, along with many others prior to this time, reaffirmed that being honest and humble in expressing our faith is vital.

I understand how awkward it can be to move from a place of private and personal faith to one of boldness, so I'm not talking about being pushy and overbearing but instead being both forthcoming and sensitive in love. Let's not be afraid to let others know that we are people of faith. Often the simplicity of saying this very thing will instigate a conversation, if not at the time, perhaps later on down the road. Once you've expressed your position, just be led by the Spirit as to what, if anything, should follow.

We're not selling Jesus. We're sharing. If we scare folks off then we've become a detriment to the faith, and that's not a good thing.

We're not selling Jesus. We're sharing. If we scare folks off then we've become a detriment to the faith, and that's not a good thing.

There's no particular formula for effectively sharing your faith, and you probably have your own evangelism style, but because I've seen it done well and also seen it executed poorly, I'd like to offer up a couple of suggestions. The best way to speak into someone's life is to have a relationship with them. When we know people and they know us, there's a greater chance they'll be open to us and the gospel. When a non-believer approaches me with a personal problem, if appropriate, I'll say, "the only way that I'd know how to help with that would be to share from a place of faith, and I don't know how you'd feel about that."

More often than not, this is acceptable to them because they likely trust me enough to share their hearts with me, or they wouldn't have asked for my help in the first place. Remember, in most cases we don't know their experiences with faith or religion prior to our discussion, so we should exercise discernment, being wise yet not wavering in what we know to be true.

We must be transparent about our own questions and struggles yet confident that in Christ, we have found freedom, love, peace, or whatever it is that has fuelled the conversation. At times we come across those who are argumentative and itching for a fight. In these cases, I endeavour to not engage, disallowing myself from being drawn into a debate.

> Early in my faith, I would have felt the need to defend God, but as time has passed, I can see that God is pretty good at taking care of Himself!

When speaking with a stranger about the things of God, we need to listen intently both to what the person is saying and also to what the Holy Spirit may be revealing to us. Perhaps we will receive a word of knowledge or be able to provide them with some prophetic insight. Maybe we'll simply be given the opportunity to meet a need. There are many creative ways to evangelize, but the main ingredient is love. What people crave is love, to be noticed, and to matter.

In Scotland, I had a great discussion with a complete stranger, a taxi driver. After establishing the reason for our move, I just left the topic alone, but he didn't. He wanted clarification.

"Are you religious?" he queried

"No, my faith is about relationship and not religion," I answered.

More curious than ever, he asked "So how does that work?"

"Well," I began, "I know Jesus personally. He's my Lord. I love Him and serve Him, and He loves me more than I could ever love Him." I went on to share what it looks like to live for Jesus. Throughout this entire explanation, I allowed for purposeful gaps should it be too much for him and he require an escape hatch! He didn't want out. He wanted more!

He told me he wasn't a Christian and he'd only been to church a couple of times; once he found it dry and boring, but the other time he felt as though "the Reverend" was speaking right to him.

"He probably was!" I replied, which seemed to surprise him. "Have you heard of the Trinity—the Father, Son, and Holy Spirit?" I continued. Indeed, he had. I explained how the Holy Spirit would have prompted the pastor to speak on something or refer to something that would touch his spirit. He was fascinated.

As we approached my destination, he shared with me that he'd be attending a funeral later on in the day, and that I was the third or fourth person he'd met over the past few days who "knew God." He was wondering what it all meant. I asked for his name, told him I'd keep him in my prayers, and he thanked me. Now that is the perfect example of a person to whom God is speaking and also a great illustration of how God provides us with opportunities to share our faith.

> It is God who draws people unto Himself, not us.

When someone has reached the point of being open, willing, broken, and anxious to hear the truth, and has a softened heart, then we have discovered a soul that God is calling into relationship. We are now God's vessel to share with them, as led.

For those who haven't yet come to this place, it's unlikely that we'll be able to make even a small dent in the wall they've built around themselves. We could actually cause them to withdraw from God even further if we're not sensitive. Again, this is my perspective, based on my experiences.

Being bold is good, but it must also be accompanied by sensitivity. Another key to evangelism is healthy "persistence." This doesn't mean chasing them down but consistently showing unconditional love. If God prompts us to pray for, help, or mentor someone, then let's be persistent in befriending them. We need to be slow to quit or give up on those whom God has put in our path. My dad excelled at going out of his way to ensure that the "invisible" ones had been "seen," not only by him but by the One who created them. He made everyone feel as though they were significant.

> The best way to share the love of Christ is to love.

I've told many a non-believer who was going through a difficult time that I would be praying for them. I can't recall having ever received a negative response. I've also discovered that it's even more effective to *ask* if they would like prayer. What I believe happens is that when someone says "yes" to prayer, a key word is spoken and subsequently heard in the heavenly realm. They have opened up a piece of their heart to God, to Jesus, and to the Holy Spirit in having given permission for prayer. That's the power of words, something I'll speak more on soon. This also shifts them into the position of seeking rather than being pursued.

We all know what it's like to be hunted down and cornered by an overzealous salesman or an evangelist from another faith (or even our own). It's awkward and irritating. Let's not present Jesus to people this way. If they've agreed to prayer, then use some discernment in determining whether to pray with them right on the spot, wait, or simply pray for them on your own. Whatever seems right at the time is likely right, but commit to praying for them and remember to ask God to protect them and the seeds planted in Jesus' name. One other point to keep in mind is the need to remain humble. While people have questions and we have found the answer in Jesus, we shouldn't be prideful.

> While we needed Jesus in the past,
> we still need Him today.

This is why Christians are often viewed as hypocritical or even offensive by non-believers. They see our imperfections and are put off when we stand before them as though we think ourselves better. None of us is worthy, not *one*! Unfortunately many Christians do believe themselves to be better! Ouch! I remember a speaker from the US saying, "Why is it that the longer we are Christians, the less we think we need Jesus?" Again, ouch! We need Jesus as much as the lost do, and if we think we don't, then we ourselves are lost. We have been saved by grace and not by any other means. We don't deserve salvation any more than the next person. No good deed or well-lived life brings us into relationship with Jesus. Let's maintain a position of humility, confessing our ongoing need for Jesus. I've found that people respond best to hearing the good news when we are truthful, honouring, and authentic. Transparency is key, and choosing our words wisely is imperative.

POWER OF WORDS

Words have astonishing power! With words, God called the world into being! We stand on God's Word and believe that God keeps His Word, as it is written. This is our bread. This is what sustains us and brings us life. We are justified by our words, and by our words we are condemned. Words can be used to speak life or death. They can be used to build up or to rebuke. Thoughtless words can cause us to put away our dreams, while words that edify will encourage us beyond what we'd ever thought possible. That's big! Many folks don't recognize the weight words carry and how vital it is that we watch the words with which we have stood in agreement.

When we agree with something someone has said, and those words aren't godly or edifying, we may have inadvertently cursed another person. Unfortunately, gossip is one of those sins that people don't take too seriously, making it one of Satan's more effective and frequently utilized weapons. Once again, scripture says that death and life are in the power of the tongue. We have all found ourselves in awkward situations in which potentially hurtful conversation abounds, causing us to repent after the fact, remorseful at having participated. So while this is a somewhat universal issue, it doesn't make it any more right or less damaging. We are still in error. Scripture says we will give an account for every idle word we speak. Did you catch that? For every idle word, we will give an account. That's quite something, isn't it? This is why I'm addressing the subject, because the harm that can be done to us and to others is far more devastating than what we may realize.

Unfortunately, I've witnessed Christians who celebrated the losses, hurts, or demise of their brothers or sisters in Christ.

After one of our bigger concerts, word spread quickly that it had been a financial disappointment. What occurred next was something one might expect from a schoolyard bully. I'm not referring to an insensitive child but rather a respected Christian woman who quite literally jumped for joy, squealing with delight at our loss. It was particularly strange behaviour, given that she was fairly affluent and we were struggling to make ends meet.

At first I felt upset and distrustful, but then God prompted me to pray for her. In the beginning, the prayers were simply carried out in obedience, but as time passed, it became evident, even to me, that my heart toward her had softened.

About two years after the initial offense, she surprised me by offering our family some items that we needed for our home. Then, over time, prayers of support were added, and eventually she even worked as a volunteer at one of our events. If you had told me that this sort of transformation and reconciliation would have taken place, I would have been dubious at best, but there it was!

> It re-established in my heart the tremendous power of prayer.

It also caused me to contemplate the reason for such joy when loss or a fall occurs within the body of Christ. I think that when one believer in a group is called to step up and out, it makes his or her friends very uncomfortable. Those watching may begin to see God's hand of favour, blessing, and protection on this person, and they immediately think to themselves "Why is that? This person isn't better than me. This person isn't perfect. Why is God using them?"

I'm reminded of the story of Joseph and his brothers. His brothers would rather see Joseph dead or sold than to see him blessed! Can you imagine? What seems to happen is that the onlookers believe they've somehow been abandoned by their brother, friend, or acquaintance, so they begin to speak out words of hatred. In so doing, they have cursed them.

Now if bad things happen to their friend, they're actually happy. If their friend encounters trouble, they criticize all the more, saying, "I told you that would happen." Well, yes, they actually spoke it into being. They feel justified in their bad behaviour, confident that this trial will slow down or stop their friend's progress, which it probably did. How tremendously sad is this! I find it bewildering that often these people aren't even interested in taking a step like the one their friend has, so why be so hateful?

Those who tear others down, who stand on the sidelines, spitefully attempting to destroy the dreams of others, have no real interest in doing something positive themselves. They have lost their way, and they've also crippled the work of the godly. What a mess! Do you see what I mean about Satan's stronghold within the church family? Those who choose to remain on the sidelines need to guard against the urge to judge, criticize, or hold others back. Not only is the one who is living by faith carrying a greater burden, but they are also on the enemy's radar, making their plight for Him all the more difficult.

I would encourage you to avoid becoming a tool in Satan's hand. I've watched in dismay the lack of grace shown to those who have stepped out of their comfort zone with a desire to be obedient and then stumbled or fallen. Have the saints forgotten that they too have received grace? Why so quick to condemn those who have succumbed to the pressures of the world whilst desiring to serve. I'm not saying that those who have sinned, fallen, or simply stumbled hold no accountability or responsibility, but the gossipers are making things more difficult.

> It's often the Christian friends or "on-lookers" who allow the enemy to use them in despicable ways.

They have fallen into a trap set by the enemy. While they ridicule and judge the one who has been hurt or fallen, they don't recognize that they've not only aided in it through word-curses or other means, but that they themselves have also fallen. Worse yet, their fall can't even be attributed to godly activity, but quite the opposite! They've actually sided with the enemy by acting or speaking on his behalf. No one wins, except the devil.

Don't allow yourself to fall into this trap. The next time you feel compelled to say, "I told you that would happen," think about what that statement means. It could mean that you actually helped to make it happen—making you a part of the problem, not a part of the solution. Remember that you will be judged by the same measure you have judged. It has a boomerang effect, so be vigilant and self-aware.

If you really feel that you must express yourself about something, then *please*, prior to doing so, diligently seek the Lord in prayer and in the Word. Ensure that your heart, thoughts, and motives are clean and pure. Sometimes the judgment or "sense" in our hearts about another person is actually about us! It could be Holy Spirit conviction that's been placed within us, intended for our own refinement and not, in fact, meant for another. Search yourself before speaking out potentially hurtful words. There have been occasions when I've been given a word of caution or rebuke that didn't line up with what God was showing me. I prayed for clarity, and in more than one case, it turned out that the word given was either intended for the person who gave it to me or was a word of warning to me, in reference to the one who had spoken it to me!

> Those who prophesy only prophesy and know in part.

They may indeed have a word for you, but they may also be prone to tossing in a couple of their own thoughts—fleshly thoughts, not spiritual thoughts. The most powerful prophetic words I have received in my lifetime have been from strangers. These words were accurate and struck a chord, demonstrating to me that they were from the Lord. It's always best to exercise caution before speaking, making certain that our words impart grace to the hearers.

It's also important to watch when, where, how, and why we use scripture in our prayer lives. I know that sounds strange, so allow me to share some revelation in relation to this concept. I'm going to use Isaiah 54:17a as my example: *"No weapon formed against you shall prosper, and every tongue which rises against you in judgment you shall condemn. This is the heritage of the servants of the Lord ..."*

I've heard many people incorporate this scripture into their prayer lives, changing and inserting words to make it more personal (for example: no weapon formed against *me* shall prosper). Many don't notice that the scripture speaks of *"every* tongue" that rises against us. When you pray this, you could be heaping judgment and condemnation upon yourself, given that you're praying against "every" word that has been spoken against you. "Every word spoken against you" would include the words you have spoken against yourself. This prayer could also be causing judgment to come upon your spouse, children, siblings, parents, or friends for the words they have spoken against you in a moment of anger or misunderstanding.

I'm not speaking against the scripture but merely pointing out that in this instance, it might be better to request that those who are rising against you receive forgiveness rather than condemnation.

When we pray this scripture, we're usually thinking about what our enemies are saying against us, not what we're saying against ourselves or others. Even so, let's not forget that scripture also instructs us to bless those who curse. I only communicate this so that our prayers become more thoughtful and careful.

Often the words we speak into being are completely contrary to what we actually desire to see occur. When I'm frustrated or angry and say something like "Everything I do seems to go wrong," I have spoken a curse against myself. What happens next is that everything I do starts to go wrong. I blame God when in fact it's simply a self-fulfilling prophecy being realized! Again, we should make every effort to speak words of life and not death.

Use words that bless, not words that curse.

When walking by faith, there are times when it seems as though too much is coming at us from too many sources, and it's difficult to determine what is of God and what isn't. When receiving input or "advice," I've learned that it's not necessary to "judge" those giving the counsel but rather to examine their fruit. *"You will know them by their fruits ... every good tree bears good fruit, but a bad tree bears bad fruit"* (Matthew 7:16a, 17).

Just as you'd likely not accept counsel on parenting from someone with no children themselves, or whose children are unruly and disrespectful, you should also carefully consider from whom you receive any spiritual input by first examining their fruit. All good fruit that you see in a person of faith is because it came from the Lord.

> *"... love your enemies, bless those who curse you,*
> *do good to those who hate you, and pray for those*
> *who spitefully use you and persecute you ..."*
> (Matthew 5:44)

Reflections

Have you ever felt under spiritual attack?

What helped you to overcome? How were you able to get through it?

Can you think of words or phrases you use that could be counter-productive to what you actually want?

NINE

Faith That Overcomes

GOD'S PLAN

I thank God that amidst the trials of life, I've chosen to make every effort to smile and maintain a sense of humour. The morning that our overseas container arrived at our very empty home in Scotland brought huge relief, but it was also a comedy of errors!

As I consumed the last of my breakfast, I felt certain that I'd heard the sounds of a large vehicle idling in front of our house. Surely it wasn't our moving truck—this was too early. One hour too early! I ran to the window and realized that it was, indeed, our truck, and with it came exceedingly tight deadlines. I was yelling for Kevin all the while hoping that our sleeping teenagers would hear my frantic cries for help and get out of bed. I went outside to speak with the driver, who told me that, as anticipated, we were only being given three hours to empty an extraordinarily full container. After that, we'd be charged an additional fee. The clock was ticking, and my heart was racing.

Determined to use our time wisely, I asked the driver to lower the back of the truck so that it would be all prepared for unloading. The driver gave me one of those heart stopping, blank, mystified gazes.

I repeated my request, explaining to him, "You see, when we packed the container in Canada, it was on the ground."

At this point I realized that the problem had nothing to do with my accent, nor did it have anything to do with his understanding my English but with the harsh reality that there was no way to lower the truck. There was no ramp, and I'm only 5'1"! This meant that we needed to unload it the way it was, numerous feet off the ground.

After recovering from disbelief at what I'd just heard, we noticed that the seal on the lock for the overseas trip needed to be removed. Of course, we had no tools (and neither did the driver!). I frantically ran inside and grabbed my recently acquired mobile to call one of our new friends for help while Kevin studied the lock, attempting to come up with a plan to remove it. Fifteen minutes passed before our very sweet, seventy-five-year-old friend arrived, decked out in coveralls and a boot full (trunk full) of tools. Bless him!

As he and Kevin madly worked to remove the seal, the kids got dressed, and I paced and prayed. This whole process took about forty minutes of our precious time. Now, with less than two-and-a-half hours remaining, we had to lift everything out of the truck, which was about four feet above the ground, with only two, Kevin and our son, being fully capable of this feat for more than half of what was in the truck. This was challenging, humorous, and traumatic all at the same time, but we got the job done, and with ten minutes to spare.

Now imagine this: the truck is driving away, and our yard, carport, and sidewalk are completely littered with furniture, musical instruments, nearly two hundred boxes, and more, all strewn in and around the smallest abode Kevin and I have ever called home since getting married and, well, you get the picture! We could almost hear the neighbours bemoaning the fact that some unhinged foreigners with a lot of "rubbish" had just moved into the area.

> Given that there are no basements, only attics or lofts, small doors and entranceways, we couldn't even get our sofa into the house!

After numerous attempts by every available means, even through windows, we gave up and gave the oversized couch away. Hopefully someone in the Highlands is now enjoying our well-travelled sofa. During all the madness, we finally got our telephone and internet connected, which allowed us to contact family and friends. This was a huge relief, especially given the news that I'd received from home, via email, about my dad's cancer diagnosis. I was terribly frustrated by my helplessness in that situation and was beginning to experience more angst than joy. I found myself becoming emotionally drained, and although we'd seen some breakthrough, we were burdened with grief over my dad's illness and my mom's struggle in caring for him single-handedly.

We still didn't have jobs, and everything from that perspective was moving at an insufferably slow rate of speed. It was incomprehensible to us why God would choose to move us to a place where there seemed to be absolutely no work for us and not even any foreseeable opportunities that lined up with our skill-sets. We hadn't met any professional musicians and were told in no uncertain terms that what had worked in Canada wouldn't work in Inverness. We met with funding organizations, new business help groups, and key folks in the arts. Nothing positive transpired. We were continually told what we could *not* do. We were anxious for even a glimmer of hope, but none came!

There also seemed to be an onslaught of adversity, as nearly every correspondence from Canada was in relation to something tragic: deaths, relational difficulties, and on and on it went. The pull toward home was strong, and all we could do was cast our burdens on Jesus and pray—a lot. We also began to receive a very strong sense that there was still more required of us. We not only needed to lay down our lives, country, family, friends, what little financial stability we had (along with everything we'd known), but

> He also wanted us to lay down our dreams,
> our gifts, and abilities too.

This was about all we could take! I was gripped by an overwhelming sadness that resulted in a personal death. We pacified ourselves with the fact that we hadn't come this far to not go the distance. We also recognized that this wasn't simply refining, but it was also testing. Were we prepared to literally lay it all down, regardless of the cost? Yes, we were, but even so, it was a devastating time and a painful process. *"Until the time that his word came to pass, the word of the Lord tested him"* (Psalm 105:19).

A period of mourning ensued as we laid down not just our gifts and abilities but the passion we had to serve God with those gifts, knowing that He wanted to do a new thing. We didn't know what that new thing was, only that it was necessary that we die to, and let go of, how we had been used in the past so that He could accomplish His goals in His way and not in ours. It was imperative that we release the past, knowing that God can make a road in the desert, creating something wonderful out of nothing at all. We had to trust that God was going to finish what He had started. Despite our best efforts, we still, on occasion, found ourselves questioning if we had heard correctly.

Was Inverness actually the place God had chosen for us?

Then, as if right on cue, we heard from Kevin's mom. She was overcome with excitement. Apparently, she had come across a very old locket she had received as a child. Upon closer scrutiny, she noticed a small bit of paper peeking out from beneath the cotton under the locket, something that in seventy years she had never before seen! She carefully unfolded the delicate and yellowed paper, which turned out to be a clipping from an old newspaper. It was an obituary that revealed some stunning information. What this seemingly insignificant little piece of paper revealed was something so crucial that we never again questioned our location!

What she read knocked her (and our) socks off. She discovered that her great-great-grandfather had lived and died in … wait for it … Inverness! Now how wild is that? Most of the focus up until this time had been on my ancestry, on my grandparents, both of whom were from Huntly, which is about sixty miles from Inverness. What this meant was that unbeknownst to us, God had sent us directly to the very city of Kevin's heritage with absolutely *no* prior knowledge of this critical piece of information! This was completely God working in hidden ways that we never could have conjured up on our own! As one friend so aptly put it:

"God writes the best stories."

How true! And they are the best because He's breathed life into them, and His fingerprints are all over them! This extraordinarily precious gift had been left unwrapped, not to be revealed until this moment in time as an encouragement to us that we were indeed in the correct location and that we had heard from the Lord!

It's tremendous that we received this piece of good news, because the word from my parents continued to be discouraging. We were praying for my dad's healing, and strength for my mom, and we were running out of money with each passing day. We were barely hanging on and then yet another attack, almost like a repeat of what we'd seen before: angry notes from a friend about our decision to move, our call to live by faith. This was something they felt had put our family in serious jeopardy. The timing couldn't have been worse. Of course, I knew in an instant that this blast of judgment was simply a fleshly response from one who didn't understand, but it was still hurtful. It caused me to reflect on all the questioning and persecution we'd received since venturing out in faith.

Friends wondered why we'd been called to a depth of faith that required we endure these hardships and they hadn't. That's a difficult one, because only God can respond to a question like that. There could be any number of reasons, the most obvious being that *all* Christians are actually called to a deep commitment of faith, but many have opted out. One thing I do know is that I have had a blessed life with a rich and wonderful childhood. I didn't have to spend the second third of my life recovering from the first part of my life. That isn't to say that I haven't had my share of struggles, but it's apparent that I've been given much, and therefore much has been required of me.

> *"For everyone to whom much is given,*
> *from him much will be required ..."*
> (Luke 12:48)

In terms of the hardships, I still believe that trouble comes as part and parcel of the faith walk. We're required to live in obedience, and although there may be difficult days, it's all about knowing and trusting that God has it in hand. That said, there have been many occasions when my husband and I have put ourselves "out there," believing in faith, waiting for our God, our source, to show up, and He's been late! Okay, let me clarify that: He's been late from my perspective. Obviously, we're still alive and well. We're still here, so He must have done something along the way to rescue us, but frequently it wasn't according to our liking or our timelines. It was, however, according to *His* plan.

Despite my best efforts to squelch any and all negative feelings, I could feel anxiety rising in me. The rent was due, and we absolutely didn't have it. We were trusting in faith, but time was up! This would be the second month in a row we'd been unable to pay! I shuddered to think what the landlord would say when I broke the news to him. I felt like such a terrible witness and reprimanded myself, heaping shame and guilt on top of the existing humiliation.

This man had been so good to us. Just the fact that he'd allowed us to move in without jobs and with no UK history and no bank account was extraordinary, but now we were asking for something over the top. We were asking for grace! Thank the Lord that my fears of being homeless and on the street lifted when this remarkable man, yet again, extended favour and also understanding.

Days and weeks passed; in fact, almost another full month went by before, at long last, God provided! I couldn't contact the landlord fast enough. I told him that a friend had given us a gift so that we could pay all the rent money owed. He was genuinely touched and told us what incredible friends we had. This we knew, but then he said something completely unexpected. He told us he admired us and the lives we were living. What? How could this be? I had convinced myself that our testimony was abysmal, but God was proving me wrong.

I've often wondered what it must have been like for Mary and Martha when their brother Lazarus took ill. They sent for Jesus, and by all accounts Jesus was late—very late—because by the time He arrived, Lazarus had been dead four days. But as the Bible shows us, Jesus got there in time! Given the length of time that Lazarus had been in the tomb, there was no doubt as to his status. When Jesus brought him back to life, the Father was glorified even more than if Jesus had simply healed him. This was clearly more magnificent! This was how God chose to realize His plan in this particular instance.

I think that Mary and Martha must have felt it would have saved them a lot of grief if Jesus had just shown up when they wanted Him to show up. At times like these we must remember our God is a sovereign God and not one to be manipulated. He knows and decides what is best.

For a couple who isn't very materialistic or money-oriented, we've cried out to God more than our fair share about this very concern. I've often moaned about the level of sacrifice that's been required and have absolutely detested how it has attempted to steal my time, my joy, and my focus. I've even found myself concerned with how, by living on the edge, we would ever be able to leave our children an inheritance. I frequently remember telling God that I had reached the end of myself, begging for help, and still nothing would change. Finally, one day I could take it no longer. I wept and prayed,

> "I'm at the end of my rope, Lord, and I don't want you to
> give me more rope like you always do. I need revelation
> so that I can get past this. It's been ten years of scraping
> by, and I can't take it another day."

Finally, after so much pain and suffering, I received insight. Until I trusted Him without reserve, He would not trust me with any further assignments or people or anything!

> I had to trust in faith, day in and day out, week in and
> week out, for Him to provide for our every need: our
> food, our rent, and for our bills to be paid!

Because I had to believe for these everyday needs, in faith, I couldn't be double-minded at *any* time or in *any* way about *any*thing. I needed to believe with all assurance that He would care for us, even though in the natural it looked impossible. I had to give up worrying and being self-sufficient and completely humble myself before God. Whoa! Here we were in a new country amidst virtual strangers, or people we'd only known for a very short time, and I needed to trust that we'd be cared for.

Well, He's good to His Word, and although in the natural we were long past the point of being on the edge, He really did take care of us. I can honestly testify that it was the first time since beginning this walk of faith that I'd had little to no worries or anxieties in terms of provision. Through this entire season, we had no backing, no credit cards, and no financial support of any kind—but we did have God!

> Once we had jumped off the edge of the cliff and found ourselves in that inexplicable free fall, although frightening to the naked eye, it was freeing to the soul.

Even when our needs mounted, and in the flesh it appeared as though the problems before us were too great to bear, I focused on Christ and His sacrifice. I thought of Moses and all those who were with him in the desert. God fed about three million people every day for forty years. I understand that was calculated to be approximately 1,500 tons of food and 11 million gallons of water, each and every day. Their clothes never wore out and their sandals always fit! I figured if God was able to do that, then He'd be able to feed, clothe, and provide shelter for our little family, which He did and does! *"And my God shall supply all your need according to His riches in glory by Christ Jesus"* (Philippians 4:19).

Clink. Clank. Clunk. Coins were being emptied into an old chipped and somewhat unremarkable mug that had found its place on the counter in our bright, cheery little blue and white kitchen. The mug was meant to contain bus fare for our kids so that they could travel to and from school on the city bus.

A friend had stopped by and noticed that it was once again empty. Although our friend had very few resources himself, he had donated to the cause! This was something that seemed to have become a regular occurrence: money anonymously popped through our mail slot, new friends stopping in to drive us to the store to collect some groceries, or even coming by to mow the lawn. There were even occasions when a local church (not our own) arranged to have groceries delivered to us! Surprise lunches and warm invitations to go sightseeing were aplenty! The generosity overwhelmed and humbled us.

We had come with hearts to help and serve and instead found ourselves being helped. I later realized that we were actually sowing into one another's lives. We needed each other, and while the situation was contrary to our nature, it was pleasing to the Lord.

THE BODY

"In the world you will have tribulation; but be of good cheer, I have overcome the world" (John 16:33b). Living in this world can be difficult, but how could it be any other way? After all, the world operates one way, and those of us who are in Christ live, think, and believe something diametrically opposed. So as we do our best to navigate our way through life, living God's way in an environment completely contrary to His, it's not surprising that we will experience pain and difficulties. The victory comes in knowing that

> *"He who is in you is greater than he who is in the world."*
> (1 John 4:4b)

Throughout those initial weeks in Scotland, we attended a number of different churches, but none seemed like a good fit. Then one day at a medical appointment, I was pleasantly surprised to learn that my doctor was a Christian! She invited us to her church, so the following Sunday we mapped out our bus route and off we went.

We were no sooner seated in the church's meeting hall when we were greeted by one of the leaders, who quickly recognized that we had not located the church we were seeking. Well, as only God can direct these things, although it wasn't the church *we'd* planned to attend, it was the one God had destined for us! This church was full to overflowing with some of the most passionate, kind-hearted, and generous people we'd ever met. We had found our new church home.

Among these believers we were astonished to find others, like ourselves, who had been sent from the nations. Did you catch that? There were others who had been sent to Inverness—just like us! We weren't an anomaly after all! What an incredible blessing (and relief) it was to come across people, passionate for God, who had moved without jobs or homes or friends, but when asked to go, went, just like us! It not only helped us to feel much less alone in our call and walk, but it was exciting to consider the possibilities of what God was doing. Natives of Scotland, those who'd arrived from other nations as led, and those of us from other nations who had "re-emigrated," had been assembled.

> I felt as though our commander in chief had gathered His troops, was moving us into place, and we, His trusting warriors, were anxiously awaiting further instruction.

I'm also fascinated by the fact that we are a musical family, knowing that throughout scripture, the musicians, the worshipping warriors, went before the army. I felt so blessed and humbled to be among those called to this impending move of God.

After a number of revelatory conversations with the Scots, we learned that in 1967, American missionary Jean Darnall, while living in England, had a vision of a time of spiritual awakening in the British Isles. She saw revival fires that God lighted from the top of Scotland, through the Highlands, and downward over England to land's end. Here we were, decades later, able to see many of the key components of this vision coming to fruition, bringing us even closer to this new thing God was planning to execute. We were tremendously excited!

In our flesh, we had hoped to have a clearer, more comprehensive picture of the plan and our role. Then one day while praying with our Scottish friends, we received understanding as to why God had hidden His plan from us. Ultimately, it was for our own protection, because although we had no idea what was to transpire, neither did the enemy! What a fantastic strategy! What this meant, though, was that in order for God's plan to be effective, it was up to us to live obediently and prayerfully exclusively by faith, trusting without seeing, day in and day out.

> He had moved us into a new level of faith,
> protection, and provision!

How comforting it was to see that God had clearly gone before us, preparing the people, the place, the spiritual atmosphere, and more. One of our new and very dear friends, a true "Invernesian," had also received a personally life-changing word from the Lord fourteen years prior to our appearance. She had been informed that God was planning to send people from the nations, and that her role was to pray, watch for, and welcome us. So for all these years, she'd been praying into the situation, long before having ever laid eyes on us, in faith and in anticipation of our arrival.

Throughout our time in Scotland, she and her family consistently, diligently, warmly, and generously cared for those of us who had been sent. She had been shown that we foreigners were able to provide something that those who had lived in Scotland throughout their lives could not, acknowledging that "a prophet has no honour in his own country."

This is why God was and is sending people to other nations. Often in our own home or country, our gifts can be minimized or rationalized away, ultimately resulting in God not being glorified and in our not being used to the fullest. If Jesus Himself was reduced to being seen as "just the carpenter's son" in His homeland, then how much more we? God wants to use us fully and completely, and sometimes this isn't possible in our communities or countries of origin. This being the case, He sends us to others, or others to us. He speaks of this in the book of Isaiah when he proclaims that it is the sons of foreigners who will build up their walls.

As God decidedly and deliberately moves people around, sometimes to new and faraway lands, it will stir things up! People may misunderstand what He's doing and what His children are called to, but rest assured, the Lord has a plan. We must all be watchful and mindful that we not miss out on our role in that plan, whether it's to go, to encourage, to pray, to welcome, or to help. Together, as led by Christ, we can be a part of His kingdom work.

> *"So Jesus said to them ...*
> *as the Father has sent me, I also send you."*
> (John 20:2)

While in Scotland, we were encouraged to see people from virtually every denomination gathering together to pray in groups and in ways we'd never seen before. God was at work. Many Christians went on regular prayer walks, praying through the city, over the hills and wherever sent. A group of volunteer street pastors worked in partnership with the local constabulary (police) to provide folks with a listening ear and to help keep the peace. A vibrant "healing on the streets" ministry took place every week in the town centre with members from a number of churches who worked together with a shared cause on their hearts. It was inspiring to see the unity.

> Something positively wonderful happens
> when unity exists.

When walls come down and Christians come together in agreement, we see God's power at work, making it possible for us to do and experience even greater things. In the book of Ecclesiastes, we read how difficult it is to break a threefold cord. There is strength and power in standing and working together. When we do this, I am convinced that God smiles. After all, when one member suffers, all suffer, and when one is honoured, all rejoice. It's teamwork. It's also entirely more fun when we're able to serve alongside positive, faith-filled, destiny-driven people who love the Lord.

I am so delighted to have a close-knit family. We enjoy one another's company, whether it involves sharing a meal, playing a game, vacationing, shopping, watching a movie together, spending time at the lake, working events, or, my personal favourite, playing music. To share a passion for music as a family has been such a blessing. Although we must weather the "von Andrews" jokes (*The Sound of Music* ... again?) and the fact that it's not particularly cool for youth to be playing music with their parents, it has been a really great thing!

It's a massive responsibility to raise children in a world that has turned its back on God, prayer, respect of self and others, morals, ethics, and the family unit. Teaching our kids to live faith-filled, Christ-like lives under these conditions is arduous.

To remain focused on what we know to be true, pure, right, and lovely *and* still function in this world is the goal. Our kids have flaws and struggles, just as we all do, but over the years they've been such a blessing and joy, mostly because of God's grace and partly because we've invested a great deal into them, their spiritual lives, and their sense of security. We may have struggled financially, but our children always had access to Mom and Dad. They've been given healthy boundaries, direction, consistency, love, prayer, guidance, encouragement, and more. This isn't to commend ourselves but to say that raising godly kids in this world requires diligence, time, and energy. We determined early on that the best way to have input into their lives was to be with them ... a lot!

In order for one of us to always be available, creativity, careful scheduling, out-of-the-box thinking, and sacrifice were required. Usually both parents must work in order to make ends meet. This is the way of the world's economy, so we did just that for many years, but through it all, we found inventive ways to manage our time, choosing our jobs carefully, purposefully, and prayerfully so that one of us was always around for the children.

It's not God's plan that today's young people receive the ragged remnants of our patience, time, and energy. It's the devil who is attempting to rule this world, and he's the one who has parents running here, there, and everywhere with activities, clubs, gadgets, and electronics, all of which attempt to steal us away from our children, or them away from us. Let's give them less stuff, fewer activities, and a calmer, more peaceful us!

> It's a lie of the enemy that says stuff and busyness are of more value to your children than *you* are!

When parents are absent, distracted, or exhausted, they need to stop and consider what values are being fed into their children's lives and by whom. A whole cause and effect phenomenon is going on here. Although parents may get away with being inattentive for a while, over time these choices will become apparent in the behaviour of their children. I'm convinced that it's easier to gently and lovingly shape a child along the way than it is to whip a neglected and disgruntled teen into shape later. "*Train up a child in the way he should go, and when he is old he will not depart from it*" (Proverbs 22:6). This is God's way, but again, the world operates contrary to God.

If you've been seduced into the world's way of thinking, or maybe you're in a "no win" situation that has you spiralling downwards or out of control, it could be of great value to think beyond that which has already been tried and failed. Look for God's solutions. Ask God for creative ways to solve your dilemma.

The Bible says we are aliens in this world, but the good news is that even if we don't fit here, when the time comes, we're gonna fit in heaven! In the meantime, though, we need to function here, and to do so effectively, we must remind ourselves that it's not flesh and blood (people) with whom we struggle but the principalities and powers of darkness (Satan). When living for Christ, we have overcome the darkness. That which desires to drag us down has no power over us. We must remind ourselves of this fact and endeavour to live according to the Spirit and not the flesh.

The responses of the flesh are not the same as those of the Spirit. As His children, we are required to love and forgive, to be patient and kind, not bitter, resentful, or rebellious. So while it's difficult not to be offended or hurt when attacked for our faith, especially by someone who knows the Lord, we must take the high road. We're all just a bunch of regular folk doing our best to make it through this life. Sometimes we get it right, and sometimes we don't, but as long as we keep growing and learning, we can rest assured that we will know more today than we did yesterday, and less today than we will tomorrow!

Throughout our journey of faith, we became acutely aware that God had called us to walk out a measure of faith that we had never before witnessed firsthand. Seeking and searching for direction, answers, and meaning without sight meant working through a wide range of thoughts and emotions with only the scriptures, the Holy Spirit, and less dramatic experiences from the past to guide us on our way. It meant re-evaluating how we viewed faith and then, on a daily basis, a continual dying to self. Although more was required of us than we had within us, we continued to trust that the Lord would lead us into His plans and purposes, which He did and still does.

THE COST

After only two months in Scotland, I knew that I needed to go back to Canada to see my mom and dad and do whatever I could to help with my dad, who was failing in his health. I was gifted with a return ticket, so I gratefully and sorrowfully departed, hoping that I could be of some assistance to my mom.

When I arrived at my parents' door after the twenty-three-hour journey, I was met with the startling news that my dad had deteriorated more quickly than I'd anticipated and had been taken by ambulance to the hospital *while* I was en route to Canada. What ensued were just two precious days at my beloved dad's bedside.

These are days I wouldn't trade for anything. Quietly and peacefully, after all the songs had been sung, the prayers had been prayed, and the words had been spoken, he passed graciously and courageously from this life to the next, ever and always a man whom I will love and admire until the day I join him in glory. He taught me enough to fill the pages of another book, mostly by what he modelled and who he was: a man of great faith, to whom not one person he encountered was insignificant or forgotten. He was a very real example of a man after God's own heart: faithful, loving, and courageous. I miss you, Dad! Your legacy lives on, and we will endeavour to honour you and your memory by serving, without reserve, the God of Abraham, Isaac, Jacob, and Ross!

After all the arrangements had been made, the memorial service was over, and some of the details had been sorted around, it was time for me to go. It was heart-wrenching to leave my mom, knowing that once my brother and aunt had departed, she would be on her own. Still, I needed to get back to Scotland. It had been painful for Kevin and the rest of the family left to mourn on their own, from such a great distance, this man who had impacted us all so significantly.

The international departures area was, as I imagine it usually is, a steady stream of busy travellers, some more tired than others but all with a focused determination to reach their desired destinations. I was in a fog. I sat down in a quiet area as tears uncontrollably poured down my face, memories of my dad flooding my mind and heart.

It hit me like a ton of bricks as I sat there at the Vancouver airport, remembering the look on his face as we'd left for Scotland. He had been right. The sadness he'd experienced was, as it turned out, justified. It was the last time he would see Kevin and his three beloved grandchildren. Had he known something that I'd been blind to see? My heart ached.

It was distressing to think that I would never again on this earth see him there, standing together with my mom, cheering us on, that I wouldn't be able to see that encouraging smile or never again feel the warmth and comfort that came from his reassuring hugs. My protector and prayer warrior, our patriarch and godly example, had gone on to a better place. I was grateful beyond words to have had such an exemplary father, but the intense pain as a result of this loss was real, and at least for today, it was far too difficult to contain.

I wondered how my family would be and how I would feel upon my return to Scotland after all that had taken place. Strangely, I had a sense of "coming home," and this genuinely surprised me. By the time I got back to Inverness, it was very close to Christmas, which meant I was immediately inundated with all the usual preparations of the season.

Amidst the hustle and bustle, the processing of what had just taken place and the grieving, I had a rather healing revelation from God. He spoke into my heart the reason for the urgency in getting us to Scotland prior to my dad's diagnosis. Had we known about the severity of my dad's illness while we were still in Canada, we likely would have moved to British Columbia and ignored the call to Scotland. He didn't want us to set Scotland aside. Scotland was where we needed to be, and although deeply concerned for all those we'd left behind, we knew it was necessary that we release them and entrust them to God, knowing He would care for them just as He was caring for us. Yes, the cost was dear, but we also knew that while there is a significant and undeniable cost in serving Jesus, there is also a substantial cost to serving the devil.

> *while there is a significant and undeniable cost in serving Jesus, there is also a substantial cost to serving the devil.*

I would far rather suffer while doing good than suffer while doing or serving that which is evil or faithless. As we stand firm in our faith, especially in the midst of trials, we will grow. It's easy to have faith when things are going well for us, but will we remain steadfast when our faith is tested? Are we truly willing to "go to the ends of the earth" for Him? Will we actually *do* all those things we sing about in times of worship, or are they just empty words that we say or sing but don't really mean?

> What happens when the rubber meets the road and God asks us to fit into His plans rather than us expecting Him to bless ours?

This is when we truly make a sacrifice of praise—when perhaps we don't feel like it. We've persevered through the struggles and pain. We've reaped because we've sown, and that's a biblical principle. But there is cost associated with this walk. Jesus asks us to consider if we have enough commitment to be His disciples. We need to count the cost and think about what it is to bear this cross and whether or not we are willing to leave all else and follow.

> *"For which of you, intending to build a tower,*
> *does not sit down first and count the cost,*
> *whether he has enough to finish it—lest, after he has laid the*
> *foundation, and is not able to finish …"*
> (Luke 14:28–29a)

In Matthew 10:39, Jesus says, *"He who finds his life will lose it, and he who loses his life for My sake will find it."* The bright side is that although there is a cost, in the end, we are rewarded. When we sacrifice all, we will gain all. Once I leave this earth, I *know* where I will spend eternity, and it will be with Jesus. So when counting the cost, regardless of what happens to me here on the earth, I know where I'll end up, and that makes the cost seem really reasonable!

So why walk by faith? It sounds a little scary. Yes, it can be, but there's also a whole lot of beauty in serving. There are far more things that are good and lovely in this walk than are negative. In serving and bringing glory, honour, and praise to the Father, Son, and Holy Spirit, we are blessed. He is absolutely passionate about seeing us brought into His fullness and image. The rough patches are strictly meant for our good. God would never hurt us or harm us. We are precious in His sight. We are His handiwork. We are loved, and we matter! We bring Him pure joy. He delights in us.

A number of years back, one of our daughters, who was only about two or three years old at the time, was at the playground. It was a beautiful sunny afternoon, and she was playing in the sand amidst the other children. I was seated on a park bench watching her whilst attending to our youngest. Although in plain view, she began calling for me—"Mom, Mom, Mom," over and over again, giving me no opportunity to respond. By the time I had a chance to say "yes," every other mom was now alerted to my little girl, standing in the middle of everything and everyone, her long, blonde hair blowing in the gentle breeze. Again she said, "Mom, watch me!" At this point, *everyone* was watching! Then she did absolutely nothing. Well, actually, she posed, and that was it! From that moment on, we called her our "Watch me child." It made me, and everyone else, chuckle. I think God would have loved that! He just enjoys watching us.

> We don't have to be doing anything special or spectacular for Him to take pleasure in us.

No matter our age, we make Him smile, simply because we're His children and He is our Heavenly Father. What a beautiful and comforting thought! He is all we will ever need. He is our salvation (Romans 1:16, 3:22–25), refuge, strength (Psalm 46:1), shield (Proverbs 30:5), fortress (Psalm 31:2), rock (2 Samuel 22:32–34), provider, source (Matthew 6:25), creator, maker, helper (Isaiah 40:28–29; Psalm 121:1–2), Lord of lords, King of kings (Revelation 19:16b), comforter (2 Corinthians 1:4), and that's just the beginning!

Reflections

What are your God stories? Are there times or events when you knew without a doubt that God was *fully* directing you?

Is He asking anything of you now? If so, what steps of faith are you taking?

TEN

REWARDS OF FAITH

A GOOD TESTIMONY

There is so much more to this awesome relationship, and although we have a tendency to focus on the "here and now," knowing Him is also about the redemption we have received through faith in Him (Ephesians 1:7). It's about living every moment unto eternity with Him (Romans 6:23). It's about being lost without Him (Romans 10:9–10). It's about His gift of salvation (Ephesians 2:8). It's all about Him and what He's done for us and not the other way around! Doesn't that make you want to serve Him with everything you've got? And in the end, everything you've got is everything He's given you!

We're told in scripture to obtain a good testimony so that we can share our stories and encourage one another. Hearing how God has worked in the lives of those around us has the ability to boost our faith. It blesses us and motivates us to walk out our own destinies with passion and conviction. It increases our expectancy about what God can and will do.

I love to hear dramatic conversion stories, but I more thoroughly enjoy hearing "faith" stories. I'm drawn to hearing about the work God is doing in the lives of the faithful, how they have been made overcomers in the face of adversity, and the ways in which the Lord's goodness and mercy has been revealed through them. I've noticed that many Christians are hesitant to share their stories, believing they have nothing exciting to say, or that their testimonies are boring. No! These testimonies are not boring. Just because you've never been a drug addict, a terrorist, or a victim of slavery doesn't mean that God isn't doing a miraculous work in and through you. If you've come from a solid Christian background, then you have a testimony of perseverance in the faith, and you're enjoying the benefits of the spiritual cleaning and faithfulness of those who've gone before you. Your "boring" life will hearten those who are trying to make a better life for their children. The testimony of your ancestors is part of your testimony. If you have been protected from evil because of your heritage, that is truly good news!

My conversion story at the age of twelve is a tame tale, yet I think that my adventure in faith is something worth sharing. If the only good testimony we have is our salvation story, then we have remained a baby in the faith. Let's move beyond the infant stage and into a maturity of faith that declares the immenseness and extravagance of God working in us and through us on a daily basis. The added bonus in all of this is that the more we speak about our faith, the more real it becomes to us.

In speaking it out, we build up our own faith and are encouraged. Yes, even as we listen to our own voices proclaiming His truths, we are lifted and edified, reminded over and over again of the mighty God we serve, and then, remarkably, we grow in faith! We also give way to that great cloud of witnesses who are able to add their "amen."

> God has a plan and purpose for each one of us.
> We need to determine what that plan is and then do it!

My husband and I are just regular folks who were called to a people, a place, and a purpose as directed by our Lord and Saviour, and because we obeyed, we have a testimony. As we seek after and follow Him, He provides us with information, strategy, and assignments on what I call a "need to know" basis.

When we arrived in Scotland, we were acutely aware of the fact that we had been removed from all that was familiar. Although difficult, we were also unencumbered by the usual distractions of life. This meant we were more easily able to hear and act in obedience to what was being communicated from on high. We didn't need to battle the pressures that can come from both personal and cultural expectations. As Canadians in Scotland, we were given extraordinary latitude and grace if we failed to do things the "Scottish way." This, however, didn't necessarily mean that we were doing things the "Canadian way" either. We were, quite simply, doing things God's way, obeying His directives, not weighed down by conformity based on cultural expectations or identity.

We were even liberated on a personal level because, as I mentioned before, those who were familiar with us and our gifts had inadvertently squelched our calling by seeing us as who we *were* or who they perceived us to be, rather than as who we *are* in Christ. We were also more useful in this new environment given that, as "outsiders," we had a fresh vantage point. We were able to view things from a completely different perspective than those who had become accustomed to a potentially altered or skewed reality. That which had become commonplace to the natives of this country were obvious areas of concern to those of us able to see this place or situation from a new and potentially clearer or untarnished perspective.

It's possible in our countries of origin to become blinded and lose objectivity in relation to that which is ugly or wrong, only because it's all that we know.

> It's possible in our countries of origin to become blinded and lose objectivity in relation to that which is ugly or wrong, only because it's all that we know.

For those who have been called away from the familiar, there's a tendency to be far more diligent and consistent in seeking the Lord. We were constantly seeking His face in an effort to walk out the call on our lives. The reason He had brought us to this new place was a force with which to be reckoned.

It saddens me to admit I prayed for Scotland more in a very short period of time than I had ever, over a lifetime, prayed for the country of my birth. Why is that? It's because Canada had become familiar. Its issues and problems faded into the background of my own life, my own dreams, and my own circumstances.

Since we'd arrived in the United Kingdom, I was far more focused on seeing Scotland set free, because I knew I'd been sent for a purpose, and my desire was to carry out that purpose. I hadn't only been called *to* something, but I'd been called *away* from something, motivating me to make certain that I'd realized my calling, whatever the role. Although there had been many a dark day, I grew to a place of embracing even the lows on this crazy roller coaster ride of faith.

It is here that we can celebrate a full-circle moment. We have arrived at the very place where this journey began - on the first day of that brand new year, not long after the passing of my dad. Although that was a difficult time, and while many more gruelling days followed, I'm so grateful I persevered, because the rest of the story, which I'm about to share, is what made it all worthwhile!

DREAMS AND VISIONS

Uniting with new friends from other nations, who had also arrived in obedience, all filled with faith, possessing little of earthly value but with steadfast hearts set to wholly serve and follow Jesus, was a complete blessing! Finally, after eight long, desert-like months in our new country, it seemed that God was moving, things were shifting and changing, and we'd do well to fasten our seatbelts and ready ourselves for the ride of a lifetime. There was a clearly distinctive link among the eight of us.

> We were four couples from four nations with a powerful connection and mandate beyond anything we could have imagined.

In sharing our stories, revelations, and dreams with one another, it was plain to see we were a team. This was no ordinary team but something so completely God-created and God-ordained that it was unlike anything I'd ever seen or experienced. Representatives from Australia, Switzerland, Scotland, and Canada had come together in the most remarkable of ways. We met with one another, hoping to assemble the pieces of what turned out to be the most amazing, supernatural puzzle ever!

What we saw, once it was all laid out before us, was astounding. It was as though pictures and stories and directives literally came into full view. The more we shared, met, and prayed, the more we "saw." It was obvious our coming together was far from random chance. God had called each family to Inverness, and although none of us could have predicted what

He was doing or was about to do, we were thrilled to not only watch the plan unfold before us but to actually be a part of that plan! He was establishing something brand new, and we were honoured to participate. It was evident that we needed one another, and we definitely needed daily instruction and wisdom from God in order to accomplish anything of lasting value. We were inspired, excited, and relieved!

> I think one of the most stunning components of what transpired were the dreams.

Our deep connections were initially the result of a dream, which was followed by a string of God-inspired dreams, each of which provided confirmation and information. Dreams became one of the key ways in which God communicated His plans and warnings to us. It was wildly fascinating and utterly astonishing!

It wasn't long before God asked us to venture out of our warm, comfortable sharing meetings and "go." The first call was to the hills overlooking our city. A great deal of demonic and occult activity had been taking place on these hills, which is likely why the Lord wanted us there. We agreed to the assignment, viewing the experience as a celebration of His victory, knowing full well that the battle was the Lord's. Interestingly, we understood it to be a family affair, so the idea of identifying and tearing down demonic strongholds with children present was not going to happen, but then again, that wasn't what we'd been asked to do. We'd been asked to go there and sing His praises, lifting up the name of Jesus.

> Our assignment was to declare Jesus as Lord from the high places, singing songs of worship, praying, and breaking bread (taking communion) together.

We felt an urgency to complete this assignment in relatively short order, so we decided to coordinate with like-minded, worshipping warriors from Inverness and go to the hills the following week. It's a good thing we didn't wait any longer than the week, after seeing the amount of opposition by way of confusion, misunderstandings, and a number of other personal and interpersonal "issues" that came our way. All were expected, but they were an annoying distraction. None of these things happened within the core group but amidst the onlookers. We were determined to push through and past the distractions.

How glorious it is when there is strength in numbers and when joined with like-minded hearts and souls. We were standing in agreement with the One whose plan we were called to enact in the earth. As planned, we met together to pray before dividing up into five groups to climb five different hills simultaneously. We got to the top of our respective hills, connected via cell phone, and then, in unison and in unity, moved into a time of worship. Something amazing happened. God spoke to the children! Most of the panic and warnings from the onlookers had been about the children, and here we were on the hills, with the children being blessed by supernatural encounters with the Almighty!

> This was just our introduction to another wild and wacky chapter in our journey with Jesus and the incredible blessings of serving alongside some of the most tuned-in, marvellous people we'd ever met.

The week following our act of obedience was relatively quiet. We had a distinct sense that something in the spiritual realm had shifted and that those serving Satan in the region were aware and angry about the ground that had been taken for Jesus. As expected, the enemy attempted to sweep in and discourage us, but we stood strong, supporting and encouraging one another. It wasn't long before we were blessed with a week filled with dreams and visions like never before. The extraordinary part of this was that almost every dream, linked with another dream, answered questions and revealed critical information about the future.

One night I had a dream that left me hanging in anticipation for more, only to discover that another member of our group had received a dream that completed mine! Not only that, but others had key dreams and visions that all tied in as well. There were even occasions when two people in the group had the same dream on the same night but from different vantage points. Our appetite for God was growing stronger by the minute.

Over a period of less than a week, we shared about ten such dreams and visions, along with other words, revelations, and instructions that had been received. It was humbling and awe-inspiring to be a part of a move of God like this. As a matter of fact, I was so impacted by the power of the dreams that I was later inspired to write, *Dreamland*, a rhyming children's book that explores the joys of heavenly night-time adventures!

We prayed together, read the Word, and sought the Lord, clearly able to see we had been knit together according to the Spirit; it was imperative that we stay connected in order to accomplish our part in what was intended for this place. That aspect of the job was extremely easy. These people were mature in their faith and in their ability to communicate effectively, and they were highly skilled in their areas of expertise, so working together was a joy at every moment.

As the days and weeks passed, the four couples who had bonded in the most extraordinary of ways continued to receive revelation through prayer, dreams, visions, prophetic words, and scripture. It wasn't long before we were called to step into even more. The battle was on, and strangely, the very gifting and call Kevin and I had been asked to lay down was precisely the one required for the task before us.

The worshipping warriors had been called into action!

The call to worship evangelism had remained the call on our lives, but now it looked entirely different from anything we'd previously experienced. In this case, it wasn't so much about seeing souls saved, although some were, but it was more about seeing the city set free from the many strongholds that sought to imprison its people in a state of blindness to the things of God. Our financial and musical resources were at an all-time low. We couldn't fathom how to accomplish the task before us with the limited number of musicians and supporters in our midst.

After a brief battle with my desire for absolute excellence, I realized I needed to drop the old ways and just do what was being asked of us within the existing parameters. We needed to use what had been provided—and what we had was all of us!

It's ironic that I was desperately seeking a vocalist who could manage the songs and handle the warfare, rather than just stepping up and singing myself, but I think that the combination of having at long last released the performing side of things, combined with a dash of insecurity (assuming someone else could better fill this role), caused me to be wary of stepping up and into that aspect of the calling. Regardless, the group of eight came together, pooling gifts and resources, and wouldn't you know it, we had everything and everyone needed in order to proceed.

For those of you surrounded by an abundance of people with finely tuned gifts, you need to understand the climate in which we were operating. There was very little music in the mainline churches. Let me clarify that. A large number of the churches were psalm-singing churches. If this is a new concept to you, it was also a new reality for us. Most of these churches only sang the psalms a cappella, with no accompaniment, no band, no instruments of any kind. They didn't even use an organ! Because of this, there were very few Christian musicians in the Highlands, and even fewer with the required skill sets to pull off the mission before us. It seemed as though the level of the bar was quite low. I guess it stands to reason that if hopes and aspirations are clouded and oppressed, then aptitude and proficiency will follow suit.

OVERCOMING OBSTACLES

This brings us back to the spiritual state of Scotland, which at the time was quite bleak and shocking to the group of us foreigners. I don't want to paint an overtly negative picture, because obviously, like in all places, there is beauty and then there are the dark recesses either hidden or not recognized as such.

In reality, Satanic practices were accepted as the norm and as part of the culture. Even Christians would inform me that this evil was simply part of their heritage! One could walk past a shop and watch people inside "playing" with a Ouija board or see books and pamphlets on ghosts and witches proudly displayed on the racks at the tourist information centre. Entire districts in the city, and even large companies, donned the name "druid." Houses built in these districts or by these companies would be "decorated" with upside down crosses, the sign of the devil. Folks openly walked about dressed in full-length black capes, hoods up, with white faces and black lipstick.

One particularly upsetting discovery was the meaning behind the scads of cassette tape ribbon we saw wound around the poles at dangerous intersections. Apparently, occult members gathered together and recorded curses into a tape recorder and then proceeded to pull the tape out of the cassette and wrap it around poles at these intersections, believing their curses would affect the passing traffic. Interestingly, these intersections were notorious for regular and bad accidents.

> The degree of explicitly evil activity was beyond comprehension.

We saw this firsthand when, after beginning the worship evangelism at our original venue, the restaurant owners found a tangled mess of cassette tape wrapped around their front door and even their parked car! Those practising Satanism dropped in to make their warnings known and threaten or just "sit in" as we sang and played. Interestingly, they never stayed longer than a song or two!

It was disturbing, however, to know that some of the local occult members in the region were also still practising human sacrifice! How startling to come to the knowledge that the most likely reason the United Kingdom has such a large number of missing persons who are never found is because of these overtly evil practices! We were shown houses with underground pathways to graveyards where all sorts of demonic activity occurred on an ongoing basis, and we learned of more horrors than I care to share.

Working against this was challenging. When faced with this opposition, I was reminded of a woman in Canada, saved by grace, who had previously been a self-proclaimed witch. Interestingly, this woman noted that even while serving the devil, she was always very aware of the prayers of Christians. She expressed how frustrating it was for both her and the others in the coven, because when Christians prayed against their demonic activity in power, victory, and authority, they needed to start the curses all over again! What we Christians can deal with in a heartbeat took them a very long time to try and reverse.

> It's fascinating to note that even those who serve the devil recognize that God's power is greater.
> We need to remember this!

We ought to embrace and utilize the authority that's been given us. I must, however, interject a word of caution. Please be extremely careful when dealing with anything of this nature, making certain you are well equipped and have back-up! While we do walk in authority, there seem to be different levels of authority, both within the enemy's camp and our own. If we really don't know what we're doing, or if we're operating outside of our designated authority, we could get hurt. Only do that which the Father asks of you.

Another obstacle directly in our path was religiosity, something that might be seen as residing on the opposite end of the scale yet wasn't. The wildly indoctrinated religious spirit found among so many of the church-goers was shocking. Laws, rules, and regulations were the order of the day. One friend spoke of what it was like growing up in an environment such as this. She told us that children were not permitted to play on Sundays. Public playgrounds would be closed with the swings tied up, and parents would remove all the toys in the house for fear of being excommunicated from the church if they hadn't properly observed the Sabbath. It was terrible. As a matter of fact, in certain areas of Scotland, this was still happening while we were there.

The religious spirit had literally driven people out of the churches and away from God. This religiosity was actually more unsettling than the demonic, because it was more deceptive than the blatantly obvious Satanists. A religious spirit is the demonic dressed up to look "pretty" and "safe," but it's yet another lie of the enemy. It was disconcerting to think of the number of people who faithfully attended these types of churches every Sunday, unaware of the deception. Following Jesus requires real commitment to Him and is not based around traditions and rules.

Many did not have relationship (with Jesus); they had religion (with an institution). We need to come to Jesus on our knees, repentant for our sins, with a sincere desire to follow Him. The repentance needs to be personal, sincere, and from the heart, not something we're bullied into. It's all based on love and grace, not sin and condemnation. When the church becomes more committed to judging than to the love, grace, and forgiveness found in Christ, it risks modelling an entirely flawed expression of our Lord and all that's encompassed by what He did at Calvary.

> We are required to love people—all people—regardless of
> their sins, opinions, and even their religion,
> faith, or lack thereof.

The longer people are Christians, the greater the risk that they might become a little bit self-righteous, even to the place of pointing fingers in judgment when telling people they need Jesus. Unfortunately, when this occurs, the witness is completely ineffective and even damaging, because it hasn't been executed in love. It puts us in the role of the experts who have arrived at some enchanted, idealistic destination rather than the ordinary people we are, who are also on a journey and in need of grace as much, or more, than the next guy. We don't need to pretend we have it all together, because we don't, and others know that we don't. We aren't perfect, just saved, and that's thanks to Jesus.

It was also peculiar to observe that although the programs in most of these churches had become completely ineffective and their membership numbers had dwindled down to almost nothing, they refused to consider any other way of doing or being church. What they couldn't seem to fathom was that the majority of unsaved people in the area had no interest in attending church—*period*. These people had no desire to hear what the church had to say.

The damage that had been done over the years was devastating. Doing things the same way would not work! Almost two generations had no substantial experience with church, let alone with faith. Their parents and grandparents had experienced "the church" and had cautioned their children to stay away. The number of youth attending services was diminutive and disheartening. Broken homes were the norm, and alcoholism a serious problem. A lot of work needed to be done before people would even consider re-visiting the idea of a life of faith.

A severe lack of understanding within the church as to what it means to operate under the leading of the Holy Spirit was another huge problem. Our little group of believers, who were led both by the scriptures and the Holy Spirit, made this larger group very uncomfortable. They were accustomed to certain ways of doing things, and we didn't fit with their pre-conceived notions about serving God and reaching a lost, disinterested, and even suspicious community. The non-believers of Scotland were not interested in religion, nor were they going to be attracted to God via any man-made method or program.

> The power of the Holy Spirit would draw people, change people, and transform Scotland.

Reflections

Have you ever received insights, revelation, or direction through a dream?

Do you journal your dreams?

What testimonies do you carry with you that encourage you?

ELEVEN

Active Faith

LET'S GO!

It became painfully obvious that the best way to reach the lost was to go and spend time with them. We needed to hear what they had to say and not judge them. We needed to engage with them *without* an agenda. That's right—I believe in the Word and in evangelism, but we were required to just sit with folks, love them, and trust that God would do the rest. By making ourselves accessible and available, we believed these folks would begin to see Christians and Christianity in a new light. We also knew they needed to see us regularly and consistently so that they could come to rely on us. A healthy community is established in love and built on a foundation of trust!

It was time to act! We applied ourselves to the task at hand, and in no time at all, we had located enough musicians to form a full gospel band. We'd also acquired a venue in which to play, street evangelists, a prayer team, greeters, an administrator, a website designer, and more. We realized that finding a restaurant or coffee shop that would remain open and allow us to do our thing might be a challenge, but we were determined. Thank the Lord, one agreed. It was situated amidst all the popular pubs and bars where people would congregate with a mission to drink until drunk. These were not nice, trendy pubs but places that seemed to have no redeeming qualities whatsoever, causing us to once again marvel at the miserable state of affairs and people's acceptance of this reality.

The plan was for the band to provide professional gospel music (the word "professional" speaks to the level of the role and not to payment, which was nil). The street evangelists would mingle with people both inside and outside the venue, chatting with passersby and answering any questions, while the prayer team prayed from within the coffee shop, outside on the streets, or wherever led, depending on the direction and strategy given them by God each night.

We left the venue's door open all evening so that the music could pour out into the streets and be released into the environment. In the beginning, it was rough going for all the team members, feeling as though we were slogging through a murky sludge about a mile high. But slog we did, pushing through and past all sorts of opposition and discouragement.

> Even though there were difficult days,
> there were always blessings to be found.

We didn't focus too heavily on advertising our events, given that our potential audience could be found right outside the venue door, roaming the streets. We notified a few of the recovery centres and missions but primarily trusted the Lord to send those who were meant to attend.

As anticipated, there were people God had on His heart. In fact, quite a few people were drawn by the power of the Holy Spirit and connected with us in conversation or in response to the music. This is what made it all worthwhile. Some passersby hovered at the door, while others ventured inside and stayed for a coffee. Still others couldn't get enough of the joy and the peace that permeated the room and happily spent a large portion of their evening with us. It didn't take long to see that what we were doing was not only an encouragement to the lost but also to the believers who desperately wanted to see change. The more they came out to listen or observe, the more they wanted to participate.

> As this type of evangelism was being modelled,
> those hungry to serve were quick to respond.

We could see a real boldness coming upon them. Without any prompting, they actively jumped out of their seats to welcome those who'd stopped by, generously purchasing coffees for strangers with money from their own pockets. Sometimes they donned their jackets and went outside to speak with people or prayed up and down the streets. It was exciting to see how infectious sharing the love of Jesus had become, and equally interesting to note how much these Christians genuinely wanted to be involved in something that mattered. They had a fresh determination and renewed hope to see their city revived. One of our very first Holy Spirit-drawn visitors was a young man who had ventured away from his pub buddies to stop in and see what was happening in our venue.

He looked to be about twenty-years-old and appeared a little confused as he ventured into the restaurant. He sat down at a table close to the band, settling in, unbeknownst to him, next to one of our daughters. There was something genuine about his interest in what was going on. He asked if he could look at the lyrics of our songs as we "performed." We pulled some music out of our binder for him, and I could see my daughter (also a musician) helping him follow along.

It was near the end of the evening, and although I had planned to speak with him, I became preoccupied with the business of a hurried clean-up. I glanced over and noticed others chatting with him, so I carried on with the job at hand. After dropping off one of the final loads of equipment outside, I noticed our new young friend standing there alone, evidently struggling with his fleshly desire to leave yet being held at bay by something bigger and stronger than himself. Against his natural inclination to run in the opposite direction, he allowed himself to become engaged in a conversation with me.

It didn't take long for me to discover that he was mildly intoxicated and also furious with God. I stood and listened to him as he spouted obscenities and let it all out. After a while, he calmed down, at which point I was able to ask him why he was so angry with God.

"He's letting my parents get divorced," was his quick reply. "Now my mom is all alone, and I'm mad." With that, his lip began to quiver. As he struggled to regain his composure, I asked if I could pray for him. I was surprised by his quick reply in the affirmative, followed by a bowed head. It was a fascinating dichotomy at play as we stood together in a holy moment, seeking the Lord

God Almighty for His hand to touch this young man and his family, amidst drunken revellers hooting and hollering all around us!

Our new friend became a regular, stopping in to see us throughout our time on the streets. Interestingly, the Lord still brings him to mind quite often, along with a couple who only came by just once to see us. The man appeared unaffected, but the woman was contemplative, teary-eyed, and even seemed to sing along. We wondered if she was a believer from another community, but before we had the opportunity to speak with her, they left.

Prior to leaving, she scribbled a note and left it behind. In essence, the note said, "You may think that what you are doing isn't working, but it is, and I thank you. I am lost. Please pray for me." Our hearts broke, and we were once again reminded of why we had been called to this. There were other testimonies too, and each one inspired us and helped us to remain focused on the task at hand. So many stories … so many people … so many beautiful moments, but it seemed to be a slow process.

> Then, after about six or seven weekends of worship on the streets, we sensed breakthrough!

This breakthrough coincided with a visit from a guest itinerant speaker who had brought a word for Scotland. Hosting this anointed preacher from Canada was both a blessing and a challenge. He was associated with a ministry in North America that was completely unorthodox, giving new meaning to the expression "out of the box." Even though he was in Scotland as a representative of his own ministry, as sent by God, we could see that this connection might create some problems in Scotland, but not to the full extent of the havoc actually realized.

The religious spirit was already being shaken, so when this speaker arrived, the shaking seemed to increase to new heights. Regardless of this, for those of us who had been praying for change, it was a tremendous encouragement to know that without a shadow of a doubt, something hugely significant was occurring in the spiritual realm! Apparently, we and he had exhibited the tenacity and perseverance to follow through with our part, and God had done His thing, which was the truly awesome part; now things were different. Transformation was taking place before our very eyes.

> God was completing the work He had begun,
> and things were changing!

It was fascinating to see how this persistence in the town centre had altered the spiritual atmosphere. It wasn't just the work of our team but so many others too: street pastors, the healing-on-the-streets folk, missionaries, prayer warriors, prophetic treasure hunters, and more, all of whom had been fruitful in their calling so that together we could rejoice as godly change came to the city.

Moving into a new venue was the next step for our team. With that move came an increased level of freedom and release. We welcomed the change and revelled in the love and acceptance we experienced in this new location.

It was around this same time one of our team members reminded us of a government program that had been initiated some time back. It was a campaign that focused on encouraging drinkers to take a break, clear their heads, and enjoy a cup of coffee before moving on to their next watering hole. It was a decent enough initiative but obviously hadn't been properly thought through, because until we'd come along, there hadn't actually been any coffee shops open for the sensible drinkers to adopt this idea!

Armed with a renewed sense of breakthrough, along with some enlightening data, we became influencers in the political arena. We began by encouraging the members of the Scottish Parliament to drop in to see what we were doing and then took it a step further by challenging them to allocate some resources to this initiative.

Thanks to the incredible favour of our Lord, we were able to stir these politicians and prompt them

> *Thanks to the incredible favour of our Lord, we were able to stir these politicians and prompt them to take notice of not just the problems in their city but also the potential solutions.*

to take notice of not just the problems in their city but also the potential solutions.

Excessive drinking, a lack of activities and resources for young people to keep them free from this ingrained evil, and the desperate need for healthy social activities were all concerns. These problems needed to be addressed, and we believed that by rewarding the willing owners of these coffee shops who'd agreed to remain open, positive change would result. Our plight was at long last noticed. One Member of Scottish Parliament in particular came by to see us on a couple of occasions, and not only did he listen to our thoughts and ideas, but he began to take some initiative. After he'd witnessed what was happening in the venue and saw the positive effect it was having, he became motivated to become a part of the solution.

> He had to admit that our small group from the nations
> had been able to initiate and see remarkable change come
> to the culture of the downtown core within
> a short period of time.

It was actually one small group led by one very large God! By doing what we could with what we had, things had changed in the people, in the spiritual, and in the natural. The politician could see that our clientele was as varied as one could imagine: young and old, saved and unsaved, drinkers and teetotalers, locals and foreigners. But the truly outstanding element was that during our three months on the streets, the crime rate had dropped substantially! It spoke volumes about the impact of the Spirit and His vessels.

As lasting change was becoming a reality, God had shown us that our time in Scotland was coming to a close, and we'd be moving on. We needed to pass the torch to those who would remain. It had been a ride unlike anything I'd ever experienced, and now this particular chapter, for me and for us, was coming to a relatively speedy conclusion. There were so many thoughts and emotions, so much to reflect upon, and so much to look forward to as we considered what the future might hold.

The reactions of our Scottish friends were as a single voice; they were despondent at our leaving. They had prayed passionately for years for those who would be sent from the nations. God had responded, and now it was the end of an era. It would be difficult for all of us to adjust. It had been a roller coaster fifteen months, and now it was over. Our role and assignment had been completed. We were leaving having seen a community changed, a people changed, and we ourselves were leaving changed—forever changed.

PERSEVERANCE

Seasons come and seasons go, and through it all I've grown to see patterns in how God speaks to us, uses us, and moves us. This is good. What's challenging is that I am now more quickly able to perceive when a dry or difficult season is approaching.

Although grateful to have grown in my ability to recognize these signs, it's also true that as a result of having "warred" through previous obstacles, valleys, and worries, I seem to experience the onslaught of weariness and discouragement more swiftly. The things I was easily able to combat early in my walk—things that should have become easier over time—actually became more difficult. With the passing of time, I found myself lacking the energy or the will to keep up the fight. I had developed a very bad habit of saying (usually internally) things like, "I can't do this anymore" or "I'm done." Obviously, these words were not bringing me to a place of breakthrough, but quite the opposite. At some point, I analyzed what I'd been saying, and the more I thought about it, the more I had to question what I was actually "done" with. Was I done with God? No! Was I done with faith? No! In truth, I was done with the devil. I needed to change my words and my thoughts to line up with His Word.

Let's be resolute in our walk, determined to press on through the trials that come with life, and the persecutions that come with faith. It's all part of the journey. When Jesus healed the paralytic as described in Luke 5, He admired and honoured the perseverance of the people who had "gone the extra mile" to see to it that their friend would be healed. It took a great deal of effort and ingenuity to come up with the clever strategy to climb, bed and all, up to the top of the house and then execute that plan by lowering their friend and his bed through the roof! Now that's tenacity at its finest. It's also a perfect example of what it is to bear one another's burdens and how our faith can be used to support others.

I believe God longs for us to operate from a place of love and humility, so that in spite of our circumstances, position, finances, or spiritual maturity, we might grow a right and generous heart for service. He wants us to know that we can begin to do things for the Kingdom right now with whatever we have. No matter how insignificant our contribution may appear, He will bless it and increase the value beyond anything we could have imagined.

> We can't keep waiting for some ideal day when everything or everyone will be in a perfect place or position before we step out of our own pain and begin to reach out to help another.

That day actually looks like *today*! If not, the day may never come, giving us reason, or an excuse, to never start. Sometimes people try to move directly into their call, and then when it doesn't go smoothly, they become discouraged and give up. If you've had a prophetic word spoken over you and it rings true and has been confirmed, then boldly step into that call, but keep in mind that there will be times when a number of steps may need to precede the realization of that prophecy. You may need to do what you can, where you are. You may need to choose to serve in a lesser capacity in an environment where you hope to one day live out your calling.

Take, for example, a young college graduate whose desire it is to operate a business. While a formal education will greatly assist him in his plight, the more meaningful teaching will come from observing and speaking with those who are already successfully doing what he wants to do. As the "rookie" meets with these proficient business people, surrounding himself in the desired environment, doing whatever he can, he will not only learn important lessons and strategies but will form and nurture relationships that will likely aid him in the future. He may need to volunteer to sharpen pencils and take out the trash at the beginning, but he'll be serving where he can in an appropriate environment. Through that action, God can use what he is doing to bless the activity and him!

We need to begin by doing our small part for the Kingdom and then watch God's wondrous plan unfold before our eyes as He adds the *supernatural* to what we've done in the natural. I'm not advocating doing a bunch of meaningless stuff in a fleshly way, but instead watching for opportunities in which God may wish to use us right where we are now! As we do what we can, God will lead us and transform our efforts into something more wonderful than anything we could have accomplished in our own strength.

A dear friend of mine in Scotland lived out this very principle. Back when she was a brand-new Christian, she was propelled toward a desire to do her part for the Kingdom. She desperately wanted to serve God, but because she didn't possess much materially, and spiritually she was considered to be just a baby, she realized that her contribution could appear modest. Regardless, determination won out, and she continued to seek God and watch for opportunities to make a difference. One day she read an ad for an organization that was looking for good used children's clothing.

This, she thought, *I can do!*

She was a woman on a mission. In no time at all, she had collected an impressive and weighty donation. She methodically and meticulously laundered, pressed, and folded everything, grouping items together according to size and gender. She went all out and was eager to present this gift, thrilled at having found something she could accomplish that was within her means.

She jumped into her little car, full of precious treasures for those in need, and off she went! She brought everything into the centre, elated that she could *do* something for God. However, the reception she received was far from what she'd expected or hoped. The woman collecting the goods didn't even thank her but asked her why she had "gone to so much bother." My friend explained she was a Christian who wanted to give of herself for God. The woman's response was full of disdain, sneering "You do-gooder Christians are here today and gone tomorrow." With that, my friend silently left the centre, unable to comprehend what had just happened.

After the initial shock wore off, she decided to demonstrate the love of God to this woman. She wanted her to know that Christians weren't as she'd described them, and even if unable to alter the woman's opinion, my friend was resolute in her decision to do this for God. With that, she continued to collect and bring items in on a regular basis. Churches in the area began to expect my friend to drop in frequently to pick up the clothing they were now collecting on her behalf.

One day, she received a rather remarkable gift. It was a stunning, deluxe model twin stroller. After much manoeuvring, my friend stuffed the fantastic find into her little vehicle, anxious to get to the centre, where she could reveal the beautiful stroller to the staff. As only God can orchestrate these things, she had no sooner pulled up to the centre and leapt out of the car when she ran smack dab into an extremely pregnant woman who had been told that the centre "rarely received strollers and had never been given a twin stroller." With that, my friend excitedly motioned the woman over to her car, revealing the gem in the back of her vehicle.

> She was amazed by what God had done and was doing, motivating her to an even greater level of service!

Not long after, while delivering a cot to another mom-to-be, my friend was shocked to find that this poor soul, who was nearly nine months pregnant, was living in a completely empty flat. There were a few blankets strewn on the floor where this sweet woman must have slept, but other than that, she had nothing.

Apparently, she was a victim of domestic violence who had escaped the clutches of her abusive partner and was literally in dire straits. My friend viewed this as an opportunity from God to give. So with the support of a pastor and his congregation, within a week she not only put the word out as to the need but successfully saw to it that this expectant mom's home was cleaned, painted, furnished, and filled in good time for the arrival of the baby!

My exceptional friend could never have anticipated what happened next, as gifts of furniture and other donated items continued to pour in, long after the initial need had been met. She didn't know what to do with so many things, mostly all large. She made some calls to see if she could locate a vacant warehouse, and even sought out funding streams to cover the expenses associated with storage facilities. When demand exceeded supply, God drew others who were doing a similar work together to form a partnership, which ultimately resulted in one of, if not *the*, largest growing charitable organization in all of Scotland! As a matter of fact, it was this company to whom we had given our large sofa when we first arrived, long before meeting its founder! By starting where she was, with what she had, God was glorified. Her obedient, willing heart and actions had been blessed, moving both her and the activity well beyond her capacity and into one that could only be attributed to God.

> In order to move forward, it's imperative that we take our eyes off ourselves and our own situations.

We need to remember that we are here to be used by God. He has provided us with eyes to see the needs of those around us, arms to embrace the hurting, and legs to walk alongside those who need a friend.

When we were in Scotland, an acquaintance from Europe, whom we had met in Canada, decided to come and spend time with us. We didn't know him very well, so while happy to see a familiar face, we were also a little surprised he had made the journey.

As we sat together in our tiny living room, I thought to myself, "Okay, this might be awkward." Our guest was far closer to Kevin than to me, and Kevin was busy that day and wouldn't be home for a number of hours. I was grateful to know that the kids would soon be home from school. Our guest was the first to break the silence, not with light and polite conversation, but rather with deep, heartfelt, personal, and highly traumatic experiences from his past. I was riveted and deeply moved.

He confessed he didn't know the reasons for his transparency, nor did he fully understand why he had made the trip, only that he had.

I surprised even myself with my speedy response. "I know why you're here. God sent you. He wants you to know how much He loves you, so He sent you to us so that we can assure you of this truth." Hearing and sensing the unconditional love of the Father was almost more than he could handle.

That week, like it or not, he was immersed in all that we were doing on the streets. Although it was completely foreign to him, it didn't take long before he got into the swing of things. Not only had God placed us in his life, but as only God can orchestrate these things, one of our team members spoke his language, meaning there was someone close at hand who could answer his "God" questions in his mother tongue! Amazing! The day before he left, he committed his life to Christ! How refreshing it was to care for the needs and struggles of another.

When we become too self-absorbed,
we also tend to become ineffective.

By taking the focus off our own problems and difficulties, we can be effective for the Kingdom, and our troubles evaporate into the background of a work and mission that matters to God. Over time, we find ourselves caring more about the things of God than being consumed by the things of "us." Let's be so in tune with God that whatever touches His heart, touches ours. This is what matters! If our hearts become entwined with God's, then we find ourselves caring about what He cares about. When we move into this state of being, it's as though our relationship with our Lord and Saviour becomes a partnership, and that's mind-blowing.

Reflections

Have you ever been constrained by a system or even by your own wrong beliefs?

How did you break free?

What small step of faith could you take now?

TWELVE

Understanding Faith

LESSONS LEARNED

Throughout this journey of faith, I've learned many a valuable lesson. While in Scotland, we learned how to operate in biblical community. We not only shared our lives and our hearts with one another, but we were blessed with the opportunity to care for one another in a way we had never previously experienced. It was all about manna for the day; it was not storing up for ourselves when we knew that our brother or sister down the road was in need today. The generosity amidst this group, none of whom had financial wealth of any kind, was staggering. It gave new meaning to the concept of "sacrificial giving" and "community living."

While it can be excruciatingly difficult to give when you yourself are in need, it's beyond humbling to be on the receiving end of such a gift. When someone gives out of lack, not out of abundance, it inspires. By the example modelled, we were motivated to look beyond our own state of affairs and consider the needs of others. If these people could give selflessly, then so could we. It astounded me as to how deeply our Heavenly Father loves and cares for us. At a time when we might have been wise to question our sanity, He connected us with friends walking a similar path, allowing us the opportunity to edify, support, and build one another up in the faith.

Our God doesn't want or deserve to be put into a box. If we're willing and available, He will use us. Although it's possible to become grieved by various trials, the genuineness of our faith is much more precious than gold, and ultimately, at the end of faith, we receive the salvation of our souls. We receive much more than we could ever give. Still, we must give ourselves over to a holy life lived for God.

> Our giving and serving should be purposeful
> and without bitterness or reserve, for as Paul says,
> "God loves a cheerful giver."

When we give or serve in this fashion, we will reap bountifully. I learned this in a very unusual way.

One day as I rummaged through my purse in search of my keys, I realized I had lost my makeup bag. I was upset because I didn't have the money to replace the lost items, and as a result of all my allergy/swelling issues, I desperately needed the help the makeup provided. Trust me, you know that old saying, "If the barn door needs painting, paint it!" Even after a friend offered to replace everything, I was still stewing about how stupid it was of me to have lost the bag.

Eventually my friend became frustrated with me and, almost in exasperation, presented me with insight that caused a major paradigm shift in my thinking. He said, "You know, somebody else likely needed that more than you." Immediately, I was okay with it being gone and felt completely at peace. It put a whole new spin on cheerfully and purposefully giving as opposed to begrudgingly having had something removed or taken. While the example may sound trite, the lesson isn't! Give generously, graciously, and extravagantly, even when it seems as though you have little or nothing to offer; it is "the widow's mite." Change your perception about *having* to pay bills and taxes, loss of belongings, or even having had something stolen. If we "give" and do so cheerfully, then God will bless us. This is not the world's way, but it is the way of God's economy.

I've learned to depend on God, knowing that He is my source in all things, in all ways, and at all times. There is a very real responsibility given to those who possess much. They may think they deserve this wealth because they worked for it, but this is wrong thinking. In the case of individuals and entire nations, all that we have is due to God. He's the one who has provided each one of us with unique and wonderful opportunities, favour, wisdom, and the ability to be gifted and blessed in the work we do.

If God's favour were removed, illness were to strike us down, the market dramatically altered, or a natural disaster occurred, would any of us still possess all that we currently do? If there is any hesitation in agreeing with this principle, then please read the book of Job or look at the situation in Haiti following the earthquakes, or examine the lives of those affected by the attacks of 9/11 (11/9 in other parts of the world). Job had it all until God removed His hand of blessing and allowed the enemy to wreak havoc with his life. It wasn't pretty. Humility is key, and honouring God is necessary.

Many of the godly who are blessed with abundance have often done their parts, but that could also be said of Job, or even of the poorest of the poor in a third world country. Hopefully we're all doing our best.

> When surrounded by more obstacles than opportunities,
> or when God's hand of protection and provision is lifted,
> it really doesn't matter how much we try.

All we have is because of Him and thanks to Him. In turn, that which we have is not ours to do with as we please. Just as the gifts of the Spirit are meant to edify and build up the body, so it is with finances. They are not meant to be hoarded for our own gain. It's about selflessness. In dying to self, we recognize that our lives and possessions aren't ours. Everything belongs to God.

Let's look at things from another perspective. What if those who currently live in lack were the ones with the riches? Would these people take the high road and bless others who required the help? If the tables were turned, would they bless those who once ignored them and their needs? Would they be giving and forgiving, as Joseph was with his brothers? It's easy to criticize those who may appear to be our polar opposites, but we must look at our own hearts and recognize the frailty of our own condition. None of us is above sin.

Another particularly revelatory lesson on this journey was in relation to our systems and programs. These structures, often developed by churches, governments, and other organizations, are here to help and guide. These groups provide services and functions that can be incredibly beneficial and can also serve as guideposts informing us of our progress and perhaps even teaching us new ways in which to operate. Even so, they aren't the be all and end all.

Our critics frequently voiced their concerns about us and what they perceived to be our blatant disregard for these structures. Because we aren't the ranting and raving "Let's cause a dispute" type of people, this perception seemed very peculiar to us. We hadn't vocalized anything "politically" and were far from controversial, except perhaps by our actions in relation to our obedient steps. In the beginning, I allowed the judgments of others to negatively affect me, until I grew in wisdom and understanding.

Let's take something concrete like the school system. A number of people were convinced that our teenagers were going to be irreparably damaged by our "globe-trotting." They fretted that we hadn't fully considered the ramifications of what we were doing and were concerned that this life of faith of ours would somehow damage our kids. Ironically, those who kicked up a fuss were the Christians from our own age group, while, in sharp contrast, younger Christians and unbelievers were drawn to the light and the adventure. The secular educators were also supportive and didn't believe our children would be harmed. They could see the value in all they were learning through these life experiences and weren't alarmed in the least.

God showed me that these structures and institutions are generally a good thing. They only become bad when they don't work for an individual or a family, or in a manner that permits folks to live in accordance with His will. They're bad if the agenda behind the structure is evil. If a child can't learn within the system, they need to be able to leave that system. If, in order to obey a call, one must work outside the system, then that's what must be done. I'm not speaking of lawlessness but of godliness.

> If we allow any program or system to dictate when and how or even what we do, then the system controls us and is no longer a help to us but a hindrance.

I am not against the system, but I also won't allow it to control me. I serve God and not the system or the program. We knew when God wanted us to leave Canada for Scotland, and we knew the timing of when we were to leave Scotland for Canada, neither of which suited the timelines of the school system. We chose to obey God. If God says to leave a country and it doesn't fit with the school's timetable, what do you do? Do you choose to obey God, or do you allow the system, which is supposed to be there for your benefit, to dictate your walk?

This is not meant to be contentious but rather to encourage freedom! The same is true within the church. Sometimes the programs have a tendency to take on a life of their own, causing leaders to become so caught up in them that it's nearly impossible to hear God's voice, let alone stop the runaway train in order to move in another direction if led to do so. It's far more important to remain obedient and tuned in to our King than to be so immersed in a program or idea that we become inflexible or unable to hear what's being said from on high.

Over the years, we have also broadened our perspective on what it is to be members of the body of Christ. Although our family left our homeland in obedience to a call, once settled, we became (as before) part of a larger body. We not only found fellowship with a small group, those from the nations, but also with a larger group.

The larger group was one that bore a recognizable church "title." Really, though, both groups were church, an assembly of believers. Both groups were made up of the body of Christ, and both groups were God-ordained. We loved being a part of both. Whether I'm in Canada or Scotland or someplace else, I am still a part of the body of Christ.

Regardless of the name outside the building or the home where I fellowship, I have committed my life to Christ and am part of *His* Church, with a sincere and passionate desire to serve, learn, live, grow, and worship Him among believers. I'd rather not get tied down by anything restrictive as I share what God was doing, so it's my hope that you will be able to catch the heart of what I'm saying. While God did move within the larger group, we observed something very fascinating about the magnitude of movement within the smaller group.

> The smaller group, the one comprised of folks from the nations, was more quickly and easily mobilized.

It wasn't encumbered by any processes or procedures. It was not only free to move but was also able to accomplish *much*! God allowed our small group to hear His voice clearly, without any limitations associated with religiosity, creeds, programs, directors, previous or current expectations, mission statements, or red tape. Because we weren't financially supported by a recognized organization or association, we didn't feel pressured to justify or gain approval for our moves, so we were void of the compelling need to build or create something just for the sake of busying ourselves with activities that might well be a good thing but not necessarily a God thing. It became all about reading God's Word, hearing God's voice, and obeying His directives.

We were still accountable to others, so this wasn't anything contrary to God and His design, but likely contrary to how many have come to believe mission work or ministry should look. I'm not speaking of a mutiny away from the church, unless it's "religious," controlling, or manipulative, in which case run far and fast. I love the church, because the church to me is God's people. While it's true that many institutions are no longer effective, I would be wrong to make a blanket statement that would see me inappropriately doing unto them as they did unto me. Church is not about a building or an organization; it's about the body of Christ, not separated or compartmentalized by walls, doctrines, or even geographical lines.

> *I would simply advise God's people to be solely bound to Christ rather than the organization, the plan, or the program.*

I would simply advise God's people to be solely bound to Christ rather than the organization, the plan, or the program.

I often think of how the "religious" folk responded to Jesus. They weren't able to experience all that He had to offer, teach, and do, primarily because they were too hung up on their rules and preconceived notions. As a matter of fact, Jesus performed very few miracles and taught very little in His homeland. He didn't spend much time trying to convince the learned He was the real deal. He simply went out and did what He was called to do, without their approval.

GOING DEEPER

We are *all* the body of Christ, and while one ministry may be smaller or without the same degree of structure, that doesn't speak to its validity or effectiveness. When God is in it, amazing things will happen, regardless of the surrounding parameters. When an organized body exhibits control rather than releasing its members to operate in His fullness, the results can be both disturbing and damaging. The intention is likely to make certain godly activity takes place, but in many cases, what results is a watered-down gospel and a people who have lost their zeal, passion, and readiness to serve.

As a result of the more controlling institutions, some people become disillusioned with serving at all. This is often because they've received false teaching. Sometimes this teaching claims that these folks either aren't ready or "trained" enough to be effective. The mistake here is not only in what is being said but in having listened to and trusted people rather than God. Legalism, manipulation, and control have the uncanny ability to suck the life and love out of people until they're left to sit lifeless and zombie-like in a misguided church building.

> We definitely need to be part of the body, but that doesn't mean we should be a part of denominationalism.

While we were in Scotland, there was a mini-revival of sorts. I don't even know if there is such a thing, but it's the only way I can describe what occurred in a tiny village north of us. What happened over a very short period of time shook the religious spirit in a mighty way.

An evangelist was in town preaching the gospel. The power of the Holy Spirit had drawn a number of lost, forgotten, fringe-type teenagers to one of the first meetings held by the visiting evangelist. These kids had not only shown up but had, in complete and utter abandonment, enthusiastically turned their lives over to Christ. These youth were so fired up about the power of God that word spread quickly throughout the village.

A minister from a very traditional church in town decided to slip into one of the meetings to investigate what all the hoopla was about. His plan was to sit quietly at the back of the room and observe. God's plan was different. The minister became so overwhelmed by the powerful presence of the Holy Spirit that he stepped forward to receive prayer for healing.

Now picture this: a very traditional and conservative minister having the courage to come forward for prayer in a meeting completely unfamiliar to him, when quite unexpectedly, a "mob" of teens with piercings, brightly coloured hair, and tattoos run toward him to lay hands on him and pray for him. This all took place before the evangelist could work his way through the crowd to pray for the minister himself. There was no need, though, because by the time the evangelist had made it there, the minister had already been healed by God through the hands of these new believers, who would have looked to the natural eye to be a somewhat motley crew.

You see, religion hadn't gotten a hold of these kids. They didn't know what the church saw as appropriate or inappropriate. All they had learned in a few short days was what Jesus did, so as His followers, they simply went ahead and did what He did, and God blessed it!

Over these years, of all that we've accomplished and learned, the ultimate lessons have been the simplest: to love at all times, to die to self, to give and then give some more, and to pray, trust, and obey.

> We seek God and then do whatever He tells us to do
> when He tells us to do it—period!

I believe this is what church leaders should be doing, instead of trying to replicate what God has done or is doing someplace else, or even imitating what has worked in the past. God's character remains the same, but what He asks of us changes and shifts with the seasons. I've worked with many professional artists and musicians. Some have made it their mission to try to be another (or better) Celine Dion, U2, One Direction, or Michael W. Smith, but they'll *never* do it. How can we ever be as good as, or better than, the real thing? It just won't happen.

I always urge these artists to discover who they are and then do that really, really well. The same is true for churches. You needn't imitate or compete with another church that appears to have found success. Instead, be successful in whatever God has made you to be. Then watch in awe and wonder as God begins to move, setting in motion a succession of events and blessings beyond your wildest dreams.

Another associated revelation came when we'd initially arrived in Scotland and discovered that so much of what God was asking of us was unrelated to our usual areas of giftedness, passion, and interest. We grew to understand that we are much more than our gifts and our abilities.

At first, He was clearly using us, but in a manner entirely different than ever before. Although difficult to comprehend, and at times almost impossible to live with, we realized that, yet again, God had provided us with a gift. We had been presented with the occasion to realize our Kingdom value, minus the skill-sets that had previously given us worth and value. When armed with little more than "us," we could see that, although stripped of everything we had once known or done or been, we could still be used. We could still be loved by the body and by our Saviour, not so much for what we could offer but for who we were.

This stunning discovery helped us to empathize with those who incorrectly deem their gifts as being lesser than gifts possessed by others. Because we weren't able to use ours, we began to feel useless, *but* we're not useless. No one is useless.

A good friend was preaching on this very subject one Sunday and illustrated his point by carrying an adorable baby boy to the front of the church. He asked the congregation what the infant was able to bring to the table. What was he able to offer? What was his value economically? Of course, from that perspective, this little one receives far more than he gives, but we were able to see that in God's economy, this little one held great value.

> I've learned that because we can become so engrossed
> in our gifts and talents, they can actually become a
> stumbling block as much as they can be an
> effective tool for Kingdom work.

While it's right and good to discover, grow, and develop our gifts, we mustn't receive our sense of value from them. When too wrapped up in what we see as our areas of strength, it can prove harmful, as we potentially block God from being able to use us in other ways.

I recognize this means moving w-a-a-a-ay outside our comfort zones. It stretches us into places where we don't want to be stretched, but this is perhaps where God wants us stretched. Having found ourselves in a place where virtually nothing was familiar, we needed to trust in God and be willing to allow Him to shape us at a time in our lives when one would think the majority of the moulding had already been done. Obviously, God wasn't finished with us.

For the first time in decades, I was able to view myself simply as one of the King's kids—not as a singer, concert promoter, event director, marketing manager, communications specialist, wife, mom, daughter, sister, mentor, friend, encourager, counsellor, company owner, chauffeur for the youth, or any of the other things I'd been known to *do*, but rather as a real live woman with a heart for God and His people, longing to serve Him in whatever capacity He chose.

Was it difficult at first? Absolutely! So much of who we believe we are is wrapped up in our designated title, or simply as others perceive us to be (based primarily on what we do), and not so much on the real live person inside—who breathes, laughs, cries, and hurts just like everyone else. Although a trying process, it was well worth undergoing. I would speculate this is likely the same principle as that of the rich young ruler who was unable to give up his possessions to fully serve God.

> Perhaps many of us are unwilling to give up our gifts,
> or whatever it is that might be dear to us,
> in order to serve God.

What a revolutionary thought! How could God ask us to lay down our gifts? I guess it's no different than Him asking the rich young ruler to give up His money (also a gift of God). Discover who you are without the stuff, the title, the family, the job, the ministry, the past, or whatever it is (good or bad) that may define you. Unearth who you are in Christ if these things, talents, people, or history weren't in your life.

Don't go and do anything crazy but it would be good if you could embark on an exploratory journey to find out who you are in Christ when emptied of all that has previously dictated that for you. I remember a business associate of mine who had absolutely stunning long, black hair, something she considered to be her greatest attribute. Sadly, there came a time when she required treatment for cancer, and her hair began to fall out. Imagine losing the very thing that provides you with self-esteem. It was heart-wrenching to watch, yet while devastating, it was also a gift to view herself and her beauty without the hair.

Consider the depression of 1929. As the stock market crashed, my guess is that the folks jumping out of the high-rise buildings to their deaths were those who had lost a significant amount of money and couldn't imagine how they would ever function in this world without that "security." Those who'd never had much shrugged their shoulders, fixed their eyes and hearts on the task before them, and prepared themselves for another difficult season. It was those who were defined by what they had who didn't know how to function without it, who decided to end it all. You might be thinking, *Well, money isn't all that important to me, so I wouldn't do that.* Then think of something that is, and maybe you'll appreciate how those folks felt.

I didn't even realize what singing meant to me until I wasn't able. I also couldn't fathom a life without art and culture, yet I've done just that. I'd always been the one to transport folks around (especially the young people), and then I found myself in the position of being the one who needed to receive the rides. I didn't realize the value of a somewhat prestigious career history until I was in a new country where it held little to no power or influence.

What if we lost a limb, our sight, our hearing, or worse yet, a child. Are we still useful in God's kingdom? Of course we are! My "losses" seem small in comparison, but whatever it is you might be asked to sacrifice, whatever may have been stripped away, whatever has turned your world upside down, who are you? Finding oneself in this place has the potential to knock you right off your feet, but I encourage you to remain steadfast, knowing Jesus will never leave you or forsake you.

> He is growing our character and will continue to do so regardless of how uncomfortable or inconvenient it may be to us.

He is growing our character and will continue to do so regardless of how uncomfortable or inconvenient it may be to us.

This is because He desires to bring us into His fullness and our destiny. I was speaking with a Christian radio announcer one day about some of the overtly nasty letters and emails he had received over some fairly trite issues. I asked him how he handled that sort of persecution day in and day out. He replied by saying that there were just as many letters of adoration. He'd learned to ignore both extremes.

You see, if he listened to the naysayers, he would have called it quits long before. If he listened to his adoring fans, he would have thought himself to be something pretty fantastic, maybe even invincible. He realized that neither was truth. God's truth is where it's at! So we seek for revelation of God's truth in every circumstance. We desire to know what He is trying to teach us. We pray with a sincere heart to be set free from all that is not God. We ask Him how He wants us to respond and who He wants us to become, and then, with discerning hearts, we forge ahead on this journey of faith!

Reflections

Has God put anyone in your path whom you could come alongside?

Is there someone to encourage you?

What first steps could you take to move forward with a goal, dream, or vision you have?

Can you assist someone else with their dream or vision?

Conclusion: Life of Faith

Answered Prayer

When we arrived in the UK, we had no idea why God had called us there. People still ask us if we can sum it up in a sentence, and we need to answer them with a simple, "No, but if you have a few hours, we'd love to share our story." There's no way to encapsulate all the reasons for such an experience into a one-liner. So much happened to us individually, as a family, and also through us.

I love how God multi-tasks!

When in Scotland, we were honoured and humbled to discover that God had answered many a prayer through us! Some of the bigger prayers, like those associated with the generational issues, the need for spiritual breakthrough in the land, and its subsequent effects on our own country, were more evident, but other prayers were answered too. Many of the young people we were privileged to meet had prayed for years that God would send them Christian friends, and our teenage kids became an answer to their prayers.

One exceptional sixteen-year-old had prayed for three years that he would be able to play in a youth band. When we arrived and saw there was nothing of the sort, I formed one! This young lad is grown and currently studying music and technology at university, while another member of that band continued to play with the "adult" group in the coffee shop we had planted. From what I understand, there has been a breakthrough not only spiritually but also musically in the area! Praise God!

For others, it was quite simply the boost and the encouragement they needed to carry on, pushing through and past the obstacles before them. Folks frequently told us that because of our act of obedience, our having modelled faith, evangelism, and perseverance, their prayers had been answered.

Of course, we also received many answers to prayer ourselves in having been cared for daily; we were fed, clothed, sheltered, and encouraged. We had been united with others who were also walking by faith. This was something we had longed to experience and was a blessing like none other. Not only were we able to see God at work firsthand, but we had also been delivered from an environment of accusations, bitterness, and gossip by having been sent away. We were returning to our homeland as new and different people, knowing God had touched us, and so had Scotland. Our hearts had become one with that faithful few who were passionate about seeing their nation turn to Christ. The experience had been filled with highs and lows like never before. We were leaving this land immersed in a "high." It was a time when we would have loved to stay, reminding us yet again, our lives are not our own. We belong to Christ, so we go where led.

We flew back to Canada not fully knowing where we were to settle. In the end, we felt led to British Columbia. Upon our arrival, we were faced with the stark reality that, once again, we needed to start all over. Having packed just one suitcase and one carry-on each before leaving Scotland, we had no idea it would be almost a year and a half later before we would set eyes on the rest of our belongings, which had been whittled down to less than a third of what we'd brought to the UK, and that was half of what we'd owned in the first place! So here we were, yet again, with no furniture, bedding, towels, dishes, or cutlery, moving into yet another home in another new city with nothing but a few clothes. I must say, though, it was the quickest and easiest moving day ever! We rolled our suitcases in, brushed our hands together in approval of our accomplishment, and said, "Whew, that's it; everything's in!"

Because we'd already experienced this, we knew how to cope, and we also knew God would provide, just as He had in the past, and He did.

It was our daughter's seventeenth birthday. Something deep inside of me began to hurt. Another "celebration" was upon us. It was another milestone to hold dear and another occasion in which we'd be reminded we had no gifts to give, no party to throw, no camera to capture those precious memories. I desperately wanted to do something special for her, but it was out of our hands. We managed to scrape together some funds for a cake, invited a couple of girls over from down the street, and "partied." Of course, we had no furniture and no dishes, so we gathered around the island in the kitchen and made the most of what we had. Another piece of me died that day.

Thank God for kids who aren't all about the stuff, kids who choose to laugh and love in the difficult days, kids who are able to amuse themselves creatively. Still, this was not how I'd envisioned commemorating her special day. Even so, I knew there were mothers out there who would have given anything just to share a moment like this with their children—perhaps one never born, estranged, or passed. We were here and we were together, so I dug down deep and found genuine joy.

Growing in faith had obviously grown on me and in me, so while I don't wish to diminish the anguish endured, it was encouraging to see I had become stronger in the Lord, with a larger capacity than ever before.

On a less personal note, I was also able to see my own country in a new light and was acutely aware of and disappointed by the pervading indifference to faith. It seemed as though many were apathetic in their walks, having lost their enthusiasm to follow Jesus wholly, fully, and without reserve. Although Scotland had its problems, there was a deep spiritual awareness, albeit misguided, but at least it could be found. North Americans, it seemed, had fallen into a slumber. I wanted to jump up and down and shake people, crying,

"Wake up! Wake up! We need to get mobilized!"

Little did I know at the time that twenty plus years later, there would be a shaking unlike anything any of us had ever known or experienced before. The entire world would be so aggressively shaken that there would be a seismic shift. People would turn their backs on one another, becoming completely intolerant. Oh, how I long for a culture of love, grace, and forgiveness to become our reality. How I long for Kingdom living!

I believe what's happened is that we have moved into a new age and era of God's dealings with mankind. It has become a season of exposure. Now more than ever before, we need to make very clear, succinct decisions for Him. There's no room or time to sit on the fence. He will separate the sheep from the goats, and when this occurs, it will be clearly evident who has been obedient and who hasn't. It will be obvious who has faith and who doesn't. If I have learned anything over all these years and through all these trials, it's to be obedient.

OBEDIENCE

As the famous line from *The Matrix* movie goes, "There's a difference between *knowing* the path and *walking* the path." The faith walk is about being obedient. It comes down to a concept as simple as that! This obedience won't look the same tomorrow or in a week or year, depending on what God asks of us. Nor will my obedience necessarily look the same as yours. The Creator is far too creative to work like that! Different things are asked of us at different times, and different people are called to different things. *"To everything there is a season, a time for every purpose under heaven"* (Ecclesiastes 3:1).

We must develop a close enough relationship with our Lord and Saviour that when we hear His voice, we know it. So that when something is required of us, be it small or large, we obey and we follow. In the Hebrew language, the words "hearing" and "obedience" are synonymous.

If you know in your spirit that a request has been made of you, are you going to refuse to be obedient because the reasons are not fully laid out for you? Does it matter that you don't yet have a full understanding of the plan, or are you just going to do as asked? If you're a parent, you'll understand that there are many occasions when what you require of your children is simple obedience. Sometimes there may not be time to fully explain yourself, or perhaps they don't yet have the maturity to comprehend the reasons for your requests. Bottom line, you expect that they will obey you. You need them to trust that you're not going to ask them to do something that will cause them irreparable damage. You need them to have faith that you would never purposefully hurt them. If they're hungry and you ask them to wait fifteen minutes until dinner is ready, you're aware that it will cause them a degree of discomfort, but that waiting won't mar them for life.

It's the same with God, who quite simply wants us to trust Him and do what is asked of us, whether or not we fully understand. Instructions from God carry with them more complicated ramifications in relation to our knowing or not knowing the whole picture. If we knew the entirety of His plans and could see what we were getting ourselves into, there's a strong likelihood that we would say "no." On the off-chance that we agreed, it's probable that we'd have the humanly arrogant tendency to attempt to refine the plan to suit us and our purposes.

If we're immersed in prayer, spending time with the Lord and in the Word of God, then when we hear a request or a command, we'll know it lines up with scripture, and obedience will easily follow. Despite the years and times I have felt alone in this walk, God has taught me to graciously love those who don't understand, and He has at all times provided me with true friends. *"Rejoice with those who rejoice, and weep with those who weep"* (Romans 12:15).

It's true that in following Him there will be hardships, but along with these hardships comes refining. The process of refinement, though painful, is a necessary step in our growth. Our youngest child frequently experienced terrible growing pains. We tried our best to soothe her aching legs with warm baths and massages, but it was awful to watch her writhe in pain. I was unable to stop the hurting because she needed to grow. It was part of the process. I've heard it said that

> God loves us just the way we are, but He also loves us too much to leave us this way!

Because His love for us is all-encompassing, He takes us deeper. He's interested in growing and refining that which is of value to Him, and that would be us! Scripture says that God *"will sit as a refiner and a purifier of silver"* (Malachi 3:3a). To be refined means we must allow ourselves to be placed into the hottest part of the flame. This not only sounds like agony—it is! But God doesn't simply walk away and leave us to "burn" in anguish. He watches over us until the purification process is complete. When that occurs, He's able to see His own image reflected back to Him, in us. How absolutely glorious is that? I trust this is what God is doing in my life. Although I know His work within me is ongoing, I see a light at the end of the proverbial tunnel. There's an ocean of opportunities before me. There are hundreds of thousands of people who don't yet know the love of Christ, and I stand in faith, believing that I am being shaped into a worthy, useful vessel to be used more and more for His purposes to reveal His glory.

Refined, purified, sanctified—we stand ready. Ready to commit ourselves fully to Christ and to the calling that is on our lives, ready to live a life of significance and purpose. I don't want to simply exist here on this earth.

> I want to know that while Christ has made a difference *in* me, He's also made a difference *through* me.

This may mean experiencing some discomfort, rejection, and pain. It may mean going against the flow, but in the end, it's just as Mother Teresa said: it's between me and God. He's the one I aim to please. He's the one I trust. Even since I started sharing this walk of faith with you, I've learned to trust the Lord at a much deeper level. I've seen His loving hand teaching, guiding, protecting, and providing. Deep down, I thought there would come a day when His grace, patience, and love would be stretched to the limit and He'd become weary of me, but He hasn't. He's shown me that *until* I trust Him with absolutely *everything* at *all times* and in *all ways*, He is unable to entrust me with the next assignment. And so it goes: I trust in faith, He is faithful, and my faith grows.

> Even when looking at worldly success, those who rank among the most successful are also usually those who have failed the most.

It often takes a number of attempts before we get it right. If we don't grow from our errors, then they end up becoming a succession of failures that discourage and defeat us. However, if we take something valuable away from each blunder and choose to learn from our failures, they aren't failures but lessons on the road to success. The difference between those of us who know God and those who don't is that we *know* we have a Heavenly Father who is leading us every step of the way, and He is incredibly patient and loving. If I stumble and fall, He picks me up and holds me so that I can dust myself off and endeavour to move on.

> *"... forgetting those things which are behind and reaching forward to those things which are ahead, I press toward the goal for the prize of the upward call of God in Christ Jesus."*
> (Philippians 3:13b–14)

Being required to trust Him with boldness and what might seem to be an extreme measure of faith has allowed me to see beyond that which is customary or in keeping with tradition. I hope and pray that you will be inspired to hunger for a deeper, more meaningful relationship with Jesus. He really is able to accomplish all that concerns you today. I would encourage you to have faith, be strong and of good courage and obedient to a call that will surely bring you into an adventure in faith! There's no life like it, and the dividends are everlasting! It is worth the cost.

The merry-go-round is absolutely fine, but the roller coaster is where it's at! I pray that you and I will receive whatever power the Holy Spirit will give so that we can fully, completely, and powerfully live for Him. God is not finished with me, and He's not finished with you. I encourage you to choose Christ. Choose life. Choose faith. Don't fret about the past. Receive forgiveness and make the rest of your days count, knowing that if God is for you, then who can be against you? And if you are *for* Him, then you are safely nestled in the arms of the Father of lights, who at the end of time will wipe away every tear with a guarantee of no more death, sorrow, or pain.

Let's go! Standing together, shoulder to shoulder, living with passion and love, fully surrendered to serving Jesus in all ways and at all times, so that when we come to the end of our days here on earth, we will be able to say as Paul did:

> *"I have fought the good fight,*
> *I have finished the race, I have kept the faith."*
> (2 Timothy 4:7)

And we, in turn, will hopefully hear those long-awaited words: "Well done, good and faithful servant."

APPENDIX I

SONS OF THUNDER PROPHECY

DREAMS/VISIONS BY JAMES RYLE

The following word was shown to me beginning in August 1990 as a result of three dreams I had:

FIRST DREAM

In August the Lord spoke to me through a dream. Prior to that dream He gave me a scripture, Isaiah 21:6, which says, this is what the sovereign Lord says, go appoint a lookout and have him report what he sees. When the Lord gave me that verse He said, I'm doing this in your life. I'm appointing you as lookout. You will see things, and when you see these things, you report them. I am now reporting to you what I have seen.

The first thing I saw in the dream was a flatbed trailer with a curtain behind it and two guitars on guitar stands sitting on the trailer. It looked like a stage but it wasn't a stage in a theatre; it was a mobile stage that could be moved into the streets or parks. This trailer was at a carnival or at a fairground. The two guitars were sitting on their guitar stands with the microphones in place and the curtain was there. The colour of these guitars was the most vivid, electric blue that I could imagine. They were acoustic guitars and that caught my eye; you would never see an acoustic guitar that was electric blue.

I then saw that the curtain was the same colour, and it captured my attention. As I stood and looked at it, two men came walking out from behind the curtain with sheet music in their hands. They were very excited as they looked at this, and they pointed out the different notes and the different measures, cadences and all the different features of this music. It was obvious that they could not wait to play this music. I looked over their shoulders and I could tell by looking at the music that it was a new song. It was not new like someone had just written it, but it was new in quality.

In the dreams my thoughts were, this is new like the Beatles music was new. When the Beatles appeared in the sixties it was a new sound and it took the world by storm. Whenever one of their songs came on, you would automatically turn it up; it had a special quality that caught your ear - it turned your head. It was the most arresting sound that our generation had ever heard. I remember looking at that sheet music in this dream and thinking that this music was going to be just like that, with one very significant distinction - this was of Christ. I stood on that platform thinking - [wait] 'til these people hear this song! I couldn't wait to see this happen, but the dream ended.

After I had written the dream down, the Lord spoke to me and said, I'm about to release a new kind of song in the streets. It will bring a revelation of the truth and it will usher men into my presence.

I filed that away until about a month later when I had another dream.

SECOND DREAM

In the second dream, I was taken to a large church which had a stage. There were rooms on either side of the stage. The room on the right side was the equipment room - it had pianos, microphones, speakers, cables, cymbals, and drums; it looked like a garage packed with stuff. I looked around and saw a power amplifier over in the corner. The amp was unplugged, the cord had been wrapped around it, it was dusty like it had been sitting in the corner for awhile. I dusted it off. What I then saw took my breath away. I gasped with a sense of discovery but also dread because of what I was holding in my hand. I held the power amp that the Beatles had used. I knew in that moment that this box was the source of their sound and their power.

I realized that people would do anything to have this amp. There are bands who for years have been looking for that sound - and for that power. They had been doing everything within their scope of imagination to get that power. Here it was and I was holding it in my hand. I felt hunted; I felt vulnerable; I felt that I was threatened. I knew that I could be hurt by those who would do anything for the amp. As I stood there holding it, I asked aloud this question, what is it doing here?

Suddenly I was out of the equipment room and standing behind the pulpit at this church, still holding the amp. The church had grown to five times the size that it was at the beginning of the dream. There was a balcony and the place was packed with people. As I looked at all these people (they were oblivious to my presence), a woman stood up in the middle of the church, and a light shone on her. She began singing a song of the Lord. Her voice filled the auditorium, and all she sang was this: In the name of Jesus Christ the Lord we say unto you, be saved. She sang it over and over. She would turn to her right and sing, then turn to her left and sing; then she would turn behind her and before her and sing the same thing. As I watched her sing, it was like a wind blowing on a wheat field. These people began to swoon in the presence of God and men and women were collapsing in their seats, converted to Christ, just by the power of that song. That was how the dream ended.

When I awoke, the Lord said that there was going to be a new and distinctive anointing and sound restored to music that will turn the heads and capture the hearts of men for Jesus Christ... Simply singing the truth in the name of Jesus Christ, We say unto you be saved, will release the power of His Spirit in such an awesome display that men and women will collapse in their seats and be converted to Christ. But the Lord said that a key to this will be this new anointing He is about to give to His music.

The Lord said that in 1970 He lifted the anointing for that extraordinary music that could arrest the attention of men, and for twenty years He has held it in His hand. He is about to release it again. He said that it does not belong to the world, it belongs to the church. That's why it (the amp) was in the church's equipment room, because it is part of the church's equipment. Music does not belong to Satan, but he has stolen much of it and seeks to use it for his own evil purposes. Music was given to worship the Lord but Satan has turned it for self-worship, which is the reason we tend to worship musicians, and they tend to require that people worship them. That is all part of the perversion of the fall.

True worship and true music belong to Jesus Christ. They are given to His church to serve Him with. The anointing the Lord is about to release on music is going to sweep the world in a manner like the Beatles did when they first came out. It's going to be a music that is new in kind, new in sound, arresting in its content; it will stop traffic, and it will turn men's heads and capture their hearts, but this time it will do it for the Lord.

In this dream I saw the balcony scene when the Beatles first played on the Ed Sullivan Show. I saw the kids pulling their hair, crying... That is what I saw - the same emotion, the same devotion, the tears in the eyes and that earnest look of love and adoration on the faces, but this time they were crying for Jesus! When this anointing comes on the music He is about to give His church, and His servants step forth in true service and worship to Him with these gifts, He will display the Holy Spirit in such a way that it will bring that kind of adoration to the Son of God, not to the musicians or our own self-centeredness.

I know that there can be some misunderstanding with this Beatle connection, but that is how it was related to me in the dream and I later saw this principle related in the Scriptures. Psalm 68:18 reads: You ascended on high, you led captivity captive and gave gifts to men - even among the rebellious ... The earth is the Lord's and all it contains (Psalm 24:1). It all belongs to Jesus Christ... The Lord makes His sun to shine on the just and the unjust. He makes His rain to come on the wicked and the righteous. Gifts and talents are given by the Lord, even though we may use them for evil.

We are now on the threshold of a prophesied new move of God which will be precipitated by a musical revival that encircles the world. God is going to bring praise into the streets. The choir that preceded the army of Jehosaphat will once again lift up the banners and strike the chords, only this time they will turn the hearts of men to Jesus Christ and not to themselves. They won't be saying, John, Paul, George, and Ringo, or, I'm of Paul, I'm of Apollos, I'm an Evangelical, I'm a Baptist, I'm a Catholic, or I'm a Lutheran. This time the adoration will be to one person alone - Jesus.

THIRD DREAM

I was then given a third dream. Again I was taken to this large church where I had seen the amplifier. This time the church was empty except for one man. He was up on the stage playing a keyboard and singing to the Lord. It was a beautiful song, and he was crying because of the tender exchange taking place between him and the Lord. He was writing the song right there, just making it up as he went. I was greatly moved by this song and the man's pure worship. I had a camera with me and I decided to take a picture of this to remember it. I took two Polaroid pictures that came out immediately. When I looked at these pictures I was stunned because both of them were glowing with a golden light. I looked up and I then could see it on the man. The entire platform around him was also glowing like gold. I knew that it was the anointing of God.

I went up to this man and said, Brother, look at this, but it startled him. He quickly turned the instrument off and stepped back. I said; Look at this, look at the anointing of God that's on you. He looked at the pictures only for a second, and putting his hands in his pockets, he shrugged his shoulders and started kicking on the ground shyly saying, Oh, gosh I didn't know you were here, I'm so embarrassed. As he was going on like this I just looked at him and asked what are you doing? You don't have to apologize for this - this is the anointing of the Lord.

Immediately the dream changed. I had these two photographs in my left hand and a parchment scroll in my right hand. I looked at that scroll and it was a letter written by an unknown soldier of the Salvation Army forty years ago. It was signed Unknown Soldier. I read this letter and it was a prophecy. It said that the time would come when the Lord God will release into the streets an army of worshipping warriors known as the Sons of Thunder. They will bring forth praise into the streets that will birth evangelism and praise and give many children to God.

I was duly impressed with this prophecy but I didn't know what to do with it or the photographs of the man worshipping. Suddenly the dream changed one more time. I was in the sky, about a hundred yards or so above the ground and I was over a highway. The highway was ten lanes wide and it only went in one direction. As far as I could see in both directions the highway was completely grid-locked, jam packed with Hell's Angels, shoulder to shoulder, wheel to wheel, just revving their motorcycles. I knew intuitively that this was the broad path that led to destruction; I knew that I was looking at lost humanity.

Then I saw on the side of the road, in single file, a group of motorcyclists who were the only ones moving. What caught my eye was that they were in single file and were moving in single file on the shoulder on this highway. They were headed towards a field that was about a mile and a half away. In the middle of this field there was a stone that was almost like the Washington Monument, but it wasn't that tall. It was a monolith-like stone, and I knew that these motorcyclists were headed toward it. I also knew that they were headed there for the purpose of touching it, because when they touched it they would receive power to come back and lead all of these Hell's Angels to Christ.

I felt that I also had to get to that stone, and that I had to be there when they got there. In the dream I was able to fly like an eagle, so I swooped down to get a closer look at the motorcyclists who were in the single file. I could see on the back of their jackets the words Sons of Thunder. I knew that this was the army of worshipping warriors about which the Unknown Soldier from the Salvation Army had prophesied.

I hastened over to this stone, but when I got there it was completely surrounded by officers of the law. They were locked elbow to elbow in riot gear with clubs and masks waiting for a big riot. My first thought was, Oh NO! These guys are not going to let us get near the stone. I was so grieved. Then I had the thought that all that was necessary was for this parchment and these photographs to touch that stone; if they touched that stone the anointing that this prophecy spoke of and the anointing that I saw on that man of music would be released on these Sons of Thunder. They would then be empowered to go into the streets and turn the Hell's Angels to Christ.

So I started to walk past the line, but they wouldn't let me through either! Suddenly I got an idea - I took the parchment and I folded it into a paper airplane, put the photographs down in the crease in order to sail it over the heads of the officers into the stone. I knew that I would only have one chance and that I could not miss. The stone was so large that the only way I could miss would be to fall short. This may be the most important issue for us. The only thing that can stop us is our stopping. Will we fall short or will we touch it?

I took the airplane with the photos and prophecy and let it fly. It flew as straight as an arrow. Just when it was about one foot from touching the stone the dream ended! I desperately wanted to go back to sleep and finish the dream but I could not. Then the Lord began to speak to me about it.

The Lord said that the stone which I saw was symbolic of Him (The stone which the builders rejected...), but that it was also symbolic of the monument that men have built to Him. These men now feel that they must protect that monument from the very people He is calling to Himself. The officers of the law stand in riot gear ready to defend the Lord from those that they don't think are worthy enough to come near Him.

The Lord then said; Say this to the man of music. Stop submitting to false humility. Stop apologizing for the anointing of God which is on you. There are many who in the privacy of their intimate times with the Lord sing the song of the Lord which is glorious. But when they come into the church or into the presence of people they let the fear of man choke the song. The Lord says Stop it! You do not need to apologize for that anointing. It is the glory of God that rests on you and the Lord is saying that it is now time for you to bring forth that which He has put in your heart to do. Sing the song of the Lord for the salvation of the lost. And your ministry in this will begin at the burial site of the fear of men.

The Lord said, Say this to the church: Stand in the light, lift up your voice and sing in the streets. Sing the simple message of the gospel - in the name of Jesus Christ the Lord, be saved. Lift up your voice as a witness to Christ and the Spirit of God will cause people to be converted.

The Lord said to the Sons of Thunder: I'm not endorsing a motorcycle gang. That is not my point. These are symbols which speak of the issues involved. A motorcycle is a quick, agile means of transportation and represents those who rid themselves of their excess baggage. It can go where other vehicles cannot go. The Lord is calling men and women into a ministry of evangelism that will take them places where the churches cannot go. And like the stigma associated with motorcycle gangs, there will be rejection and misunderstanding associated with this ministry. Some will not understand why they go into bars and associate with people who look demonic (and sometimes are), just as the Lord Himself was misunderstood for His associations. Even so, the word of the Lord to the Sons of Thunder was, be in the world but not of it!

Then the Lord said, Say this to the officers of the law: Put down your clubs and stop defending Jesus from people who you don't think are worthy enough to touch Him. Open your doors and let those people come in. Stop being so enamoured by the monument that you take your eyes off the living stones.

Then the Lord said this, the last call is a call to intercession. He said to me that the dream ended the way it did for an important reason. He wanted us to know that while it is going to happen, it is not happening yet. It's about to happen, and between now and when it does there is a call for intercession. When the prophecy of that unknown soldier of the Salvation Army of a generation ago and the vision of the anointed man of music are joined hand in hand by those who will intercede, and those two things touch the heart of Jesus through intercessory prayer, the anointing will be released on the Sons of Thunder. And the Sons of Thunder will be released into the streets. We will then see a worldwide move of the Spirit of God.

There are three groups that actually make up these Sons of Thunder. They are the musicians, the evangelists who are not musicians and the musicians who are evangelists. Some who are musicians are being called to be a Son of Thunder even though they are not evangelists. Some are evangelists who are being called though they are not musicians. Of course, there are some who are both evangelists and musicians. In some cases there will be musicians on a flatbed trailer, drawing the crowds for the evangelists. When the musicians who have dedicated themselves to the Lord Jesus Christ begin to play this new song, the Spirit of God is going to move in that crowd. The evangelists will touch these people and explain what is happening to them. The Sons of Thunder are both the musicians and the evangelists who work together.

The Sons of Thunder, copyright 1991 MorningStar Publications Inc.

APPENDIX II

THE GOSPEL: A LOVE STORY

*It's not what you've done, good or bad.
It's about what He's done to make it right
and you righteous.*

When I thought of those readers who may not know or walk closely with Christ, I felt that this Appendix could be helpful in bringing greater understanding. I remember being grilled by a news reporter who wanted to know my thoughts on how folks may or may not end up in hell. He persisted in interrogating me about this issue, firing questions at me, making one attempt after another to back me into a corner, apparently hoping to entice me to say something controversial that would make a good headline. Here I was trying to create a beautiful, godly celebration, and all that the journalist could focus on was trying to coerce me into saying something negative about my faith.

I quietly prayed, asking God for guidance, and then responded with, "The only way to the Father is through His Son, Jesus Christ." I wasn't interested in getting bogged down by theology and divisive arguments. I knew I needed to redirect his focus from hell and damnation to the good news part of the story, and after repeating the same answer over and over again, I was finally able to accomplish this. The real story *is* about the *love* of God and not what many see as the wrath of God.

*"For God did not send His Son
into the world to condemn the world,*

> *but that the world*
> *through Him might be saved."*
> (John 3:17)

Many prefer to focus on hell, but from what I've learned, hell was never intended for people; it was created for the devil and his angels (Matthew 25:41). Hell can be another word for the grave, and it was only because of the sin of Adam and Eve that the grave became an option for mankind. If we don't receive the gift of salvation through Christ, *we* have chosen the alternative. The choice is ours.

Again, God takes all the flack for this, but by rejecting the good news, it's we who have opted out of immediate access to life, grace, favour, and, most of all, true love. I realize this will likely upset some folks, but that's because it's uncomfortable to be faced with the fact that there are consequences for our actions or inactions. There is no sitting on the fence with God. He is gracious and long-suffering, but once we've heard the story of His great love for us, we need to make a decision.

> *"For the wages of sin is death, but the gift of God is*
> *eternal life in Christ Jesus our Lord."*
> (Romans 6:23)

We have all sinned and fallen short of His glory, yet He offers us this amazing and unmerited gift. Although we keep messing up, He just keeps on loving us, so much that He sent His only Son to become a curse on the cross in order that we might be saved. We just need to say "yes" in faith and in obedience to the one who provided us with this extravagant gift. We *can* be saved thanks to God's grace and our commitment to follow Jesus.

If you haven't yet made a decision to follow Jesus, I strongly encourage you to get whatever answers you require in order to make this commitment. God promises that if we seek, we will find. Keep seeking the truth and you will find it, and I assure you that when you find the truth, you will have found Christ.

I do feel compelled to offer up a caution. If you are seeking, don't linger too long in making this decision. Simply put, we don't know when our days here on earth will be over, and it's critically important that we live out our days and years with an absolute certainty that we will spend eternity with Jesus. It's more than okay to sincerely ask God to reveal Himself to you, but once He has made Himself real to you, don't delay in turning your life over to Him. The enemy would love to see us engulfed in the academia of it all when, in the end, what's required of us is child-like faith.

> *"... Assuredly, I say to you, unless you are converted and become as little children, you will by no means enter the kingdom of heaven."*
> (Matthew 18:3)

We needn't complicate this. Jesus didn't come to condemn but to save. He desires that none should perish and that we would all receive salvation. God loves us so much that He sacrificed His own Son for us. If you're ready to make a decision and would like to know and follow Jesus Christ, you need only acknowledge that you believe Jesus lived and died and rose again, that He is the Son of God, and that you want to live your life for Him. Ask God to forgive you of your sins, to cleanse you, heal you, and release you from all that would hinder you from living a life of freedom. Invite Him to reign in your heart and pray that He protect you from all that's not Him. It's as simple as that. If you do this, then you will *know* that you have begun an incredible journey following our Lord and Saviour, Jesus Christ!

If you made this decision today, allow me to be the first to welcome you into the family of God! While the walk won't always be easy, you will absolutely never regret having made this decision. Celebrate and experience the joy of the Lord to the fullest! Continue to walk with Him all the days of your life, and you will spend eternity in His presence. How radical is that? We serve an amazing God, and now you're a member of the body of Christ! This is not the end but simply the beginning.

You will need to get your hands on a Bible and start the process of uncovering the truths and lessons found in God's Word. The most recommended section of the Bible for new believers is the book of John, the fourth book of the New Testament, so that's a great place to start. As you grow in knowledge and understanding, you'll be motivated to go out and make disciples of others, encouraging them to be followers of Jesus too. Get connected to other believers and also learn about water baptism and the baptism of the Holy Spirit. Congratulations on the best decision of your life!

Also by Deborah J. Andrews:

The children in your life will absolutely adore the rollicking rhythms and captivating imagery as night-time adventures come to life through God-inspired dreams!

To order *Dreamland* or additional copies of this book, please visit: www.deborahjandrews.com.

www.ingramcontent.com/pod-product-compliance
Lightning Source LLC
Chambersburg PA
CBHW071311110426
42743CB00042B/1267